FIFTH EDITION

PRIVATE PILOT SYLLABUS

by

Irvin N. Gleim, Ph.D., CFII

and

Garrett W. Gleim, CFII

ABOUT THE AUTHORS

Irvin N. Gleim earned his private pilot certificate in 1965 from the Institute of Aviation at the University of Illinois, where he subsequently received his Ph.D. He is a commercial pilot and flight instructor (instrument) with multi-engine and seaplane ratings and is a member of the Aircraft Owners and Pilots Association, American Bonanza Society, Civil Air Patrol, Experimental Aircraft Association, National Association of Flight Instructors, and Seaplane Pilots Association. He is the author of flight maneuvers and practical test prep books for the sport, private, instrument, commercial, and flight instructor certificates/ratings and is the author of study guides for the sport, private/recreational, instrument, commercial, flight/ground instructor, fundamentals of instructing, airline transport pilot, and flight engineer FAA knowledge tests. Three additional pilot training books are *Pilot Handbook*, *Aviation Weather and Weather Services*, and *FAR/AIM*.

Dr. Gleim has also written articles for professional accounting and business law journals and is the author of widely used review manuals for the CIA (Certified Internal Auditor) exam, the CMA (Certified Management Accountant) exam, the CPA (Certified Public Accountant) exam, and the EA (IRS Enrolled Agent) exam. He is Professor Emeritus, Fisher School of Accounting, University of Florida, and is a CFM, CIA, CMA, and CPA.

Garrett W. Gleim earned his private pilot certificate in 1997 in a Piper Super Cub. He is a commercial pilot (single and multi-engine), ground instructor (advanced and instrument), and flight instructor (instrument and multi-engine), and he is also a member of the Aircraft Owners and Pilots Association and National Association of Flight Instructors. He is the author of study guides for the sport, private/recreational, instrument, commercial, flight/ground instructor, fundamentals of instructing, and airline transport pilot FAA knowledge tests. He received a Bachelor of Science in Economics from The Wharton School, University of Pennsylvania.

Gleim Publications, Inc.
P.O. Box 12848 · University Station
Gainesville, Florida 32604

(352) 375-0772
(800) 87-GLEIM or (800) 874-5346
FAX: (352) 375-6940

Internet: www.gleim.com
Email: admin@gleim.com

ISSN 1097-1785
ISBN 1-58194-488-8

First Printing: July 2006
Second Printing: March 2011

This is the second printing of the fifth edition of
Private Pilot Syllabus
Please email update@gleim.com with
PPSYL 5-2 in the subject or text. You will
receive our current update as a reply.
Updates are available until the next edition is
published.

EXAMPLE:

To: update@gleim.com
From: *your email address*
Subject: **PPSYL 5-2**

ACKNOWLEDGMENTS

The photograph on the front cover of the Liberty XL2 is courtesy of Liberty Aerospace.

The authors appreciate the assistance of Mel Carpenter, Professor of Aviation, Florida Community College at Jacksonville, and the many FAA employees who helped in person or by telephone.

HELP!!

This is one book in a series of five books, listed below, designed specifically for persons who aspire to earn a private pilot certificate.

Private Pilot Syllabus
Private Pilot Flight Maneuvers and Practical Test Prep
Private Pilot FAA Knowledge Test
Pilot Handbook
FAR/AIM

Please send any corrections and suggestions for subsequent editions to the authors, c/o Gleim Publications, Inc. The last page in this book has been reserved for you to make comments and suggestions. It can be torn out and mailed or faxed. Alternatively, you may email your comments and suggestions to aviation@gleim.com.

Also, please bring this book to the attention of flight instructors, fixed-base operators, and others interested in flying. Wide distribution of this series of books and increased interest in flying depend on your assistance and good word. Thank you.

NOTE: UPDATES

Send an email to update@gleim.com as described at the top right of this page and visit our website for the latest updates and information on all of our products. To continue providing our customers with first-rate service, we request that questions about our materials be sent to us via email, fax, or mail. The appropriate staff member will give each question thorough consideration and a prompt response. Questions concerning orders, prices, shipments, or payments will be handled via telephone by our competent and courteous customer service staff.

TABLE OF CONTENTS

IF FOUND, PLEASE CONTACT
Pilot Name _____
Address _____
_____
_____
Telephone # _____
Email _____

PREFACE

Thank you for choosing GLEIM. Our training materials (books, software, audios, and online) are intuitively appealing and thus very effective in transferring knowledge to you. The Gleim system saves you time, money, and frustration vs. other aviation training programs.

This syllabus will facilitate your studies and training for your private pilot certificate.

1. Please read the following Introduction carefully.

2. The "Lesson Sequence and Times" section on pages 6 and 7 shows ground lessons being completed as you complete flight lessons. We encourage you to work ahead in your ground lessons and begin them (and even complete them) prior to beginning your flight training.

3. Completion of your flight training in 35 or 40 hours is unrealistic. Most individuals take 50+ hours. Thus, many, if not most, of our 26 (or 28) flight lessons will take more than one flight to complete. The "checkoff" boxes to the left of each lesson item provide for up to three flights. Your CFI should write in any additional flights if they are needed.

   The OBJECTIVE is to develop "PTS level" proficiency as quickly as possible. "PTS level" means that you can perform at the level required by the FAA's Practical Test Standards (PTS).

4. Homework consists of about 1,200 pages to read and/or study in your Gleim *Private Pilot FAA Knowledge Test* book, Gleim *Private Pilot Flight Maneuvers and Practical Test Prep* book, Gleim *Pilot Handbook*, and the Pilot's Operating Handbook or Operating Limitations for your airplane. Each flight lesson also directs you to review topics and material studied for previous lessons. The Gleim *FAR/AIM* book is for reference.

Why is the GLEIM SYSTEM different? It focuses on successful completion, as quickly and as easily as possible. The requirements for earning your private pilot certificate are listed beginnning on page 2. This syllabus facilitates your flight training so you achieve a "PTS level" of proficiency on 50 FAA "tasks" as quickly as possible!

GO FOR IT! Start studying for your FAA knowledge test today. Reference Study Units 1 through 11 in *Private Pilot FAA Knowledge Test* and *Pilot Handbook*. Start studying for your FAA practical test by reading Chapter 5 (of Part I) in *Private Pilot Flight Maneuvers and Practical Test Prep*.

We have an easy-to-follow and easy-to-complete study system. From the very start, we want you to focus on success. This means answering over 80% of the FAA knowledge test questions correctly AND being able to explain and demonstrate the 50 FAA practical test tasks to your CFI at a "PTS level" proficiency.

Enjoy Flying Safely!
Irvin N. Gleim
Garrett W. Gleim
March 2011

INTRODUCTION

This syllabus is a step-by-step lesson plan for your private pilot training. If you are not familiar with the basic requirements of the Federal Aviation Administration (FAA) private pilot certificate, please read pages 2 through 5 in the *Private Pilot FAA Knowledge Test* book and pages 3 and 4 in the *Private Pilot Flight Maneuvers and Practical Test Prep* book. This syllabus is intended to be used in conjunction with the following four Gleim books:

Private Pilot Flight Maneuvers and Practical Test Prep
Private Pilot FAA Knowledge Test
Pilot Handbook
FAR/AIM

Your flight instructor will fill out the included Flight Training Record as you complete each flight lesson. The Flight Training Record should remain at the flight school as a record of your progress.

WHAT ELSE DO YOU NEED?

If you purchased this syllabus as part of the Gleim **Private Pilot Kit**, you will need to purchase (1) a local sectional chart and (2) an *Airport/Facility Directory (A/FD)*. They are published every 6 months and 56 days, respectively. You will need a current copy of each for your FAA practical test. Gleim does not include these publications in your kit because there are 37 different sectional charts and seven different *A/FDs* for the conterminous U.S.

Additionally, you will need to purchase a copy of the Pilot's Operating Handbook (POH) (sometimes called an Information Manual) for the make and model of your training airplane. Alternatively, you may make a photocopy if a POH is not available for purchase.

REQUIREMENTS FOR PRIVATE PILOT CERTIFICATE

There are a number of requirements to earn your private pilot certificate. The final step is your FAA practical test, which will be conducted by an FAA examiner. Your practical test will consist of an approximately 1-hour oral exam followed by a 1- to 2-hour flight test. You will be well prepared for your practical test by your CFI and your Gleim pilot training materials. In addition, you must meet the following requirements:

1. Obtain a combined FAA medical certificate/student pilot certificate.

    a. Your medical exam will be conducted by an FAA-designated aviation medical examiner (AME).

    b. Ask your CFI or call your local flight school for the names and telephone numbers of the AMEs in your area, or visit our website at www.gleim.com/aviation/amesearch.php for a listing of AMEs by state and city.

    c. A copy of FAA Form 8500-8, *Application for Airman Medical Certificate or Airman Medical and Student Pilot Certificate*, appears on pages 87 and 88.

        1) Make a copy of Form 8500-8 and fill out items 1 through 20 to reduce the amount of time at your AME's office.

2. Pass your FAA pilot knowledge test, which consists of 60 multiple-choice questions and is administered at an FAA-designated computer testing center. You will attend one of hundreds of computer testing centers after you have prepared for your test. Everything you need to prepare for your FAA pilot knowledge test is in your Gleim ***Private Pilot FAA Knowledge Test*** and ***Pilot Handbook*** books. Gleim ***FAA Test Prep*** Software Download and/or **Test Prep for Windows Mobile** will facilitate your study. (To find out exactly what to expect from the computer testing center of your choice, use *FAA Test Prep* Software Download's convenient vendor emulation testing format.) We have estimated 35 hours for complete preparation for your pilot knowledge test. You may turn to page 4 for instructions on how to begin at any time.

3. Undertake flight training as described in Lessons 1 through 25 beginning on page 30. Many of the lessons will require more than one flight to complete. We also have provided space for your instructor to record extra flights within each lesson as needed to make you comfortable and proficient.

The KEY TO SUCCESS in your flight training, which also minimizes cost and frustration, is your study and preparation at home before flying with your flight instructor. The more you know about flying, flight training, and each flight lesson, the better you will do.

4. PASS your FAA practical test. See Part I, Chapter 5 in ***Private Pilot Flight Maneuvers and Practical Test Prep***.

    The further you study (not just read) in ***Pilot Handbook*** and ***Private Pilot FAA Knowledge Test*** to prepare for your FAA pilot knowledge test before you commence your flight lessons, the better! Studying in advance will enable you to feel at ease and confident while meeting with several flight instructors or visiting a number of flight schools to select the program that is best for you. We have provided an introductory flight page in our syllabus to log introductory flights. Have each CFI make a logbook entry on page 85 for each introductory flight.

    The importance of home study certainly applies to piloting. Do NOT show up at the airport expecting to be spoon-fed by your CFI. If you do, your flight training will be slow going and frustrating.

    It's fun to be successful! Be overly prepared before you get to the airport for each flight lesson.

HOW TO PROCEED

1. If you are reading someone else's copy of *Private Pilot Syllabus*, obtain a Gleim **Private Pilot Kit** from your FBO/flight school/bookstore, or call (800) 874-5346 or visit www.gleim.com for publisher-direct service.

    The kit is a flight bag containing *Private Pilot FAA Knowledge Test* book and *FAA Test Prep* Software Download/**Test Prep for Windows Mobile**, *Pilot Handbook*, *Private Pilot Flight Maneuvers and Practical Test Prep*, *Private Pilot Training Record*, *FAR/AIM*, *Pilot Logbook*, a flight computer, a navigational plotter, and this *Private Pilot Syllabus*.

2. Read this Introduction (12 pages).

3. Obtain your medical/student pilot certificate. Tell your aviation medical examiner that you wish to receive a student pilot certificate, not a regular medical certificate.

4. Begin preparing for your FAA private pilot knowledge test. Read the Introduction (18 pages) in *Private Pilot FAA Knowledge Test*. Plan on passing your test within 30 days. Use your Gleim books, *FAA Test Prep* Software Download/Test Prep for Windows Mobile, and/or Online Ground School. See the Introduction in *Private Pilot FAA Knowledge Test* for specific instructions.

5. Select a CFI and/or flight school. See Part I, Chapter 1 in *Private Pilot Flight Maneuvers and Practical Test Prep*. Use page 85 (in this syllabus) to have your CFI log any introductory flights.

    a. You may want to search our CFI Directory at www.gleim.com/aviation/cfi/search/.

6. Begin your flight training, scheduling at least two lessons a week. Prepare thoroughly at home for each flight lesson. See the flight training syllabus in this book for details on your flight lessons.

PART 141 VS. PART 61 SCHOOLS

Federal Aviation Regulations (FARs) list the requirements to obtain your private pilot certificate. Flight schools can conduct your training by following either FAR Part 141 or FAR Part 61.

A Part 141 flight school is issued a pilot school certificate by the FAA after applying to the FAA and meeting certain requirements. A Part 141 flight school's syllabus is approved by the FAA during this certification process. Thus, if you are using the Gleim *Private Pilot Syllabus* in a Part 141 flight school, it must be used in your training.

The majority of flight schools, and flight instructors not associated with a flight school, provide the required training as specified under Part 61.

The major difference between Part 141 and Part 61 training is in the minimum amount of total flight time and solo flight time. Generally, a Part 141 school is more regimented than a Part 61 school; thus, the FAA set the minimum flight time at 35 hours under Part 141 and 40 hours under Part 61. However, the 35- vs. 40-hour minimum requirement is NOT relevant because most people require 50 to 60 hours to complete their private pilot training.

You should select a flight instructor and/or flight school that you are comfortable with rather than being concerned with whether the training is conducted under Part 141 or Part 61. This syllabus meets the requirements for either Part 141 or Part 61.

The Gleim syllabus has been reviewed by the FAA in Washington, D.C., and found to adequately meet the requirements of a syllabus under Part 141 or Part 61, as appropriate (see FAA letter on the back cover). Thus, the Gleim *Private Pilot Syllabus* can be used by any Part 141 school with minimum effort. We suggest that the school write a letter to its FAA inspector advising the FAA of the school's intent and the names of students who are going to be trained under this Gleim syllabus.

If a Part 141 school cannot or will not use this syllabus, consider finding another Part 141 or Part 61 school for your training OR please call (800) 874-5346 if you have questions or problems.

GLEIM *PRIVATE PILOT SYLLABUS*

This syllabus consists of a ground training syllabus and a flight training syllabus. The ground and flight training may be done together as an integrated course of instruction, or each may be done separately. If done separately, the ground syllabus may be conducted as a home-study course or as a formal ground school.

This syllabus was constructed using the building-block progression of learning, in which the student is required to perform each simple task correctly before a more complex task is introduced. This method will promote the formation of correct habit patterns from the beginning.

Ground Training Syllabus

The ground training syllabus contains 11 lessons, which are divided into two stages. The ground training syllabus meets the training requirements of FAR Part 61 and Appendix B to FAR Part 141. The ground training can be conducted concurrently with the flight training, with the ground lessons completed in order as outlined in the lesson matrix, beginning on page 6. Ground training may also be conducted as part of a formal ground school or as a home-study program.

It is recommended that the lessons be completed in sequence, but the syllabus is flexible enough to meet the needs of an individual student or of a particular training environment. When departing from the sequence, the instructor is responsible for considering the blocks of learning affected.

Each ground lesson involves studying the appropriate study unit in the Gleim *Pilot Handbook*. After each study unit is completed, you need to answer the questions in the appropriate study unit in the Gleim *Private Pilot FAA Knowledge Test* book and review incorrect responses with your instructor. You may use the *FAA Test Prep* Software Download/**Test Prep for Windows Mobile** or **Online Ground School** to answer the questions in each study unit.

At the end of each stage, you are required to complete the stage knowledge test before proceeding to the next stage. The end-of-course knowledge test is completed after the Stage Two Knowledge Test. Shortly after the end-of-course test, you should take the FAA private pilot knowledge test. These knowledge tests will refer you to FAA figures found on pages 71 through 81 and on the inside front and back covers.

If this ground training is home study, we recommend that you complete the syllabus as quickly as possible and pass the FAA private pilot knowledge test so you will have more time to prepare for your flight lessons.

Gleim *FAA Test Prep* Software Download and/or Test Prep for Windows Mobile can be used to answer the questions at the end of each ground lesson. Our *FAA Test Prep* Software Download contains the FAA figures and outlines in addition to the questions.

FAA Test Prep and Test Prep for Windows Mobile allow you to select either STUDY MODE or TEST MODE. In STUDY MODE, the software provides you with an explanation of each answer you choose (correct or incorrect). You design each study lesson:

> Topic(s) and/or FAA learning statement codes you wish to cover
> Number of questions
> Order of questions -- FAA, Gleim, or random
> Order of answers to each question -- Gleim or random
> Questions marked and/or missed from last session -- test, study, or both
> Questions marked and/or missed from all sessions -- test, study, or both
> Questions never seen, answered, or answered correctly

In TEST MODE of the *FAA Test Prep* Software Download, you decide the format -- CATS, LaserGrade, or Gleim. The software imitates the operation of the FAA-approved computer testing companies. Thus, you will have a complete understanding of exactly how to take an FAA pilot knowledge test before you go to a computer testing center. When you finish your test, you can study the questions marked and/or missed and access answer explanations.

Flight Training Syllabus

The Part 141 flight training syllabus contains 25 lessons (27 lessons if Part 61), which are divided into two stages. It is recommended that each lesson be completed in sequential order.

Stage One of the flight training syllabus is designed to provide the student with a foundation of good flying habits for his/her flying career. This stage ends with the student's first solo flight. During this stage, the student will become proficient in the knowledge, procedures, and maneuvers required for solo flight. Prior to the student's first solo flight, (s)he will complete the presolo knowledge test. The instructor is responsible for ensuring that the student meets the applicable requirements of FAR 61.87, Solo Requirements for Student Pilots.

Stage Two is designed to provide the student with the knowledge and skills required for confident, repeated solo flight, including cross country navigation. This stage also addresses night-flying and preparation for the FAA private pilot practical test. Part 141 requires one solo cross-country flight of at least 100 NM, while Part 61 requires a total of 5 hours of solo cross-country flight time, with one flight of at least 150 NM. We have included two additional solo cross-country lessons to meet the Part 61 solo time requirements. These flights are optional and need not be performed if you are using this syllabus under Part 141.

Stage checks. Stage checks are designed to ensure that the student has acquired the necessary knowledge and skill. The Stage One check (Lesson 12) is to ensure that the student is competent for safe solo flight. The Stage Two check (Lesson 25) is the end-of-course stage check for a Part 141 graduation certificate.

The chief flight instructor (Part 141) is responsible for ensuring that each student accomplishes the required stage checks and end-of-course tests. The chief flight instructor may delegate authority for conducting stage checks and end-of-course tests to the assistant chief flight instructor or a check instructor.

Stage checks will be used as a review by instructors training under Part 61 to ensure that the student has the appropriate knowledge and skills.

Sequence of a flight lesson. Each flight lesson will begin with a preflight briefing. During this time, the instructor should first answer any questions the student may have from the previous lesson. Next, the instructor will brief the student on the lesson content. During this briefing, the instructor will evaluate the student's preparation for the lesson. Prior to a solo flight, the instructor must review with the student the maneuvers to be done, the objective of the lesson, and the completion standards.

During the flight portion of the lesson, the instructor should begin with those maneuvers listed as review before introducing new maneuvers. The time required for each lesson will vary depending on the airport and the location of the training areas.

At the end of each lesson, the instructor will conduct a postflight critique and a preview of the next lesson. This time should be used to review the good points during the lesson, to identify and explain fully any problem areas, and to discuss how to correct the problems.

The length of the preflight briefing and postflight critique will vary with each student and with his/her degree of preparedness for the lesson.

Student preparation. The key to minimizing frustration and costs is preparation. You should budget an average of 2 to 4 hours of home study prior to each flight lesson. Learning will be easier when you are fully prepared so that your instructor can maximize the time spent in flight training.

PRIVATE PILOT SYLLABUS GROUND AND FLIGHT LESSON SEQUENCE AND TIMES

The Ground Syllabus follows on pages 13 through 26 and the Flight Syllabus follows on pages 27 through 57.

The following table lists the sequence of the flight and ground lessons and the minimum time for each lesson. The times listed are for instructor/student guidance only and are not meant to be mandatory times. These times will ensure that the minimum time requirements for aeronautical knowledge and flight training are in compliance either with Part 141, Appendix B, Private Pilot Certification Course, or with FAR Part 61.

Each training flight (solo and dual) must include a preflight briefing and a postflight critique of the student's performance by the instructor. This time will be entered into the logbook as "ground training."

LESSON	Page	Flight Training (Dual)	Solo/ PIC	Dual Cross-Country	Solo Cross-Country	Night	Instrument	Aeronautical Knowledge Training
STAGE ONE								
Flight 1 Intro to Flight	30	1.0						
Ground 1 Airplanes/Aerodynamics	14							3.0
Flight 2 Fundamentals	31	1.0						
Ground 2 Instruments, Engines, Systems	15							3.0
Flight 3 Instrument Maneuvers	32	1.5					0.5	
Ground 3 Airports, ATC	16							3.0
Flight 4 Slow Flight/Stalls	33	1.5						
Ground 4 FARs	17							3.0
Flight 5 Emergency Operations	34	1.5						
Flight 6 Ground Reference Maneuvers	35	1.5						
Flight 7 Review	36	1.5						
Ground 5 Performance, Weight, and Bal.	18							3.0
Flight 8 Go-around/Slip	37	1.5						
Flight 9 Review	38	1.5					0.3	
Flight 10 Review	39	1.5						
Flight Presolo Knowledge Test	58							
Flight 11 First Solo	40	0.5	0.5					
Ground Stage One Knowledge Test	19							1.0
Flight 12 Stage One Check	41	1.0					0.2	

		Flight						Ground
LESSON	Page	Flight Training (Dual)	Solo/ PIC	Dual Cross-Country	Solo Cross-Country	Night	Instrument	Aeronautical Knowledge Training
STAGE TWO								
Ground 6 Aeromedical/ADM*	20							2.0
Flight 13 Second Solo	43	1.0	0.5					
Ground 7 Aviation Weather	21							3.0
Flight 14 Short/Soft Field Operations	44	1.5						
Ground 8 Aviation Weather Services	22							3.0
Flight 15 Solo	45		1.0					
Ground 9 Navigation	23							3.0
Ground 10 Navigation Systems	24							3.0
Flight 16 Navigation Systems	46	1.5					0.5	
Ground 11 Cross-Country Flight Planning	25							3.0
Flight 17 Cross-Country	47	2.0		2.0				
Ground Stage Two Knowledge Test	64							1.0
Flight 18 Night	48	1.5				1.5	0.3	
Ground End-of-Course Knowledge Test	26							2.5
Flight 19 Night Cross-Country	49	2.0		2.0		2.0	0.4	
Flight 20* Solo Cross-Country	50		2.0*		2.0*			
Flight 20A** Solo Cross-Country	51		3.0**		3.0**			
Flight 20B** Solo Cross-Country	52		2.0**		2.0**			
Flight 21 Review	53	2.0						
Flight 22 Solo	54		1.0					
Flight 23 Review	55	2.0					0.5	
Flight 24 Solo	56		1.0					
Flight 25 Stage Two Check	57	1.0					0.3	
Part 141 TOTALS		30.0	6.0*	4.0	2.0*	3.5	3.0	36.5
Part 61 TOTALS		30.0	11.0	4.0	7.0	3.5	3.0	36.5
		Total Times						

*Part 141 requires one solo cross-country flight of at least 100 NM total distance with landings at a minimum of three points; one segment of the flight must have a straight-line distance of at least 50 NM between the takeoff and landing locations. Since no minimum time is required, we have allocated 2 hours for this flight in Flight 20.

**Part 61 requires a minimum of 5 hours of solo cross-country flight time, including one flight of at least 150 NM total distance with landings at a minimum of three points; one segment of the flight must have a straight-line distance of at least 50 NM between the takeoff and landing locations. Flights 20, 20A, and 20B are used to meet these solo cross-country and total solo time requirements. Since only 5 hours of solo cross-country is needed, Lesson 20B may be replaced with one hour of local solo practice.

EXPLANATION OF *PRIVATE PILOT TRAINING RECORD* BOOKLET

Also available separate from this syllabus is a *Private Pilot Training Record*. This *Pilot Training Record* is provided for flight schools that conduct training under 14 CFR Part 141, which requires that detailed training records be maintained for each student. When properly completed, the training record booklet will meet the training record requirements of Part 141.

Training Record Elements

The training record booklet consists of three main sections:

- The front cover contains student personal information and information about the training course.
- The back cover serves as a ground training and student evaluation record.
- The inside of the booklet consists of a two-part flight training record and a separate record of instructor endorsements.

Using the Training Record

Front Cover: The front cover of the training record should be filled out by the student, his/her flight instructor, and the chief flight instructor at the time of enrollment. Spaces provided to record credit awarded for previous ground and flight training should be completed by the chief instructor. The chief instructor also should complete the enrollment certificate (found on page 81 of this syllabus) and place it in the pocket at the back of the training record.

At the completion of training, the chief instructor should complete the information on the front cover, as appropriate (e.g., graduation, transfer, or termination). If the student has graduated, the graduation certificate (found on page 83 of this syllabus) should be completed and placed in the pocket at the back of the training record.

Back Cover: The ground training record should be filled out by the instructor after each ground lesson is completed, regardless of whether ground training is being conducted formally or as a self-study program. The time spent and date of completion should be noted and the record initialed by both the student and the instructor.

The stage and end-of-course test records should be filled out by the instructor after each stage and end-of-course test has been taken by the student, graded, and reviewed with the instructor. The date of the test, the result, and the date of the review should be noted. The record should then be initialed by the student and signed by the instructor. Each stage and end-of-course exam answer sheet should also be placed in the pocket at the back of the training record.

The student evaluation records should be filled out by the instructor following the presolo knowledge test and evaluation and by the chief instructor after each stage check. The date and result of the test should be noted and the record initialed by the student and signed by the instructor or chief instructor (the chief instructor must sign the record for each stage check).

Inside: The flight training record consists of two parts: The Flight Record is a chronological record of each training flight that is made during the course, while the Lesson Record is an itemized record of the student's performance on the lesson items listed in each specific flight lesson. The record of instructor endorsements is a record of information related to each flight instructor endorsement that is pertinent to the course of training.

The Flight Record should be used to record the following information for each flight that is performed during the course: date of the flight, aircraft make and model, aircraft registration number, flight lesson(s) undertaken during the flight (this item has been left for the instructor to complete in order to accommodate lessons that require multiple flights to complete or that must be completed out-of-sequence), initials of the instructor conducting the flight (if applicable), and the types and amounts of flight time accumulated during the flight and during the entire course to date.

The Lesson Record should be used to record the student's performance on each lesson item that is contained in the lesson(s) that were undertaken during the flight. The Lesson Record consists of 25 individual lesson records (one for each lesson contained in the syllabus). Each individual lesson record contains an itemized reprint of the lesson items contained in the corresponding flight lesson. Because it is recognized that many lessons take more than one flight to complete, each individual lesson record is designed to allow the instructor to record and grade the student's performance on each lesson item for up to six flights.

The Lesson Record should be used to record the following information for each flight lesson: the date of each flight undertaken to complete the lesson, the time spent during each pre- and post-flight briefing, and the student's performance on each lesson item. When the lesson is completed, the date of the lesson's completion should be noted and the record initialed by the student and signed by the instructor who conducted the final flight for that lesson.

The record of instructor endorsements should be filled out by the instructor at the time that each student pilot certificate and/or logbook endorsement is provided. The date of the endorsement and any applicable conditions should be noted, and the record should be signed by the instructor. The instructor's flight instructor certificate number and expiration date also should be noted.

AIRPLANE(S) AND LOCAL AIRPORT(S) WORKSHEETS

The airplane(s) worksheet on page 10 is to be used as a study reference of fuel, oil, and airspeeds for the airplane(s) you may use during your training. The local airport(s) worksheet (on page 11) is to be used as a study reference of elevation, radio frequencies, traffic pattern direction, and runway lengths at your primary airport and any other local airports you may use during your training.

AIRPLANE(S) WORKSHEET

N-number   _____ _____ _____ _____ _____

Make & Model   _____ _____ _____ _____ _____

Max. Ramp Wt.   _____ _____ _____ _____ _____

Fuel Capacity   _____ _____ _____ _____ _____

Min. Fuel for Flight   _____ _____ _____ _____ _____

Oil Capacity   _____ _____ _____ _____ _____

Min. Oil for Flight   _____ _____ _____ _____ _____

V_{SO} _____ _____ _____ _____ _____

V_{S1} _____ _____ _____ _____ _____

V_R _____ _____ _____ _____ _____

V_X _____ _____ _____ _____ _____

V_Y _____ _____ _____ _____ _____

V_{FE} _____ _____ _____ _____ _____

V_A _____ _____ _____ _____ _____

V_{NO} _____ _____ _____ _____ _____

V_{NE} _____ _____ _____ _____ _____

Best Glide   _____ _____ _____ _____ _____

LOCAL AIRPORT(S) WORKSHEET

Airport Name	_____	_____	_____	_____	_____
Identifier	_____	_____	_____	_____	_____
Elevation	_____	_____	_____	_____	_____
ATIS	_____	_____	_____	_____	_____
Ground	_____	_____	_____	_____	_____
Tower	_____	_____	_____	_____	_____
UNICOM	_____	_____	_____	_____	_____
Runway	_____	_____	_____	_____	_____
Length	_____	_____	_____	_____	_____
Traffic Pattern	Left or Right	Left or Right	Left or Right	Left or Right	Left or Right
Obstructions	_____	_____	_____	_____	_____
Runway	_____	_____	_____	_____	_____
Length	_____	_____	_____	_____	_____
Traffic Pattern	Left or Right	Left or Right	Left or Right	Left or Right	Left or Right
Obstructions	_____	_____	_____	_____	_____
Runway	_____	_____	_____	_____	_____
Length	_____	_____	_____	_____	_____
Traffic Pattern	Left or Right	Left or Right	Left or Right	Left or Right	Left or Right
Obstructions	_____	_____	_____	_____	_____
Runway	_____	_____	_____	_____	_____
Length	_____	_____	_____	_____	_____
Traffic Pattern	Left or Right	Left or Right	Left or Right	Left or Right	Left or Right
Obstructions	_____	_____	_____	_____	_____
Traffic Pattern Altitude	_____	_____	_____	_____	_____

PART 141 STUDENT INFORMATION

Enrollment Prerequisites

A student must hold a student, sport, or recreational pilot certificate prior to enrolling in the flight portion of the private pilot certification course.

Solo Flight Requirements

Before a student can fly solo, (s)he must complete the specified training, pass a presolo knowledge test, and receive the required student pilot certificate and logbook endorsements from his/her flight instructor.

Graduation Requirements

The student must complete the training specified in this syllabus, with a minimum of 36.5 hours of ground training in the specified aeronautical knowledge areas and a minimum of 36 hours of flight training (30 hours of dual and 6 hours of solo). These requirements are reflected in the Gleim Flight Training Syllabus. See page 27.

Stage Checks

The student must score a minimum of 80% on the knowledge test at the completion of each stage in the ground training syllabus and must score a minimum of 80% on a comprehensive knowledge test at the conclusion of the training.

The student must satisfactorily complete a stage check at the completion of each stage of the flight training syllabus.

Credit for Previous Training

The student may be given the following credit towards this private pilot certification course for previous pilot experience and knowledge [FAR 141.77(c)]:

1.   If the credit is based on a Part 141 training course, the credit may be 50% of the requirements for this course.

2.   If the credit is based on a Part 61 course, the credit cannot exceed 25% of the requirements for this course.

The receiving school will determine the amount of course credit to be given, based on a proficiency test, a knowledge test, or both.

END OF INTRODUCTION

PRIVATE PILOT
GROUND TRAINING SYLLABUS
AIRPLANE SINGLE-ENGINE LAND

GROUND TRAINING COURSE OBJECTIVES

The student will obtain the necessary aeronautical knowledge and meet the prerequisites specified in Appendix B to FAR Part 141 (and FAR 61.105) to successfully pass the private pilot knowledge test.

GROUND TRAINING COURSE COMPLETION STANDARDS

The student will demonstrate through stage knowledge tests and school records that (s)he meets the prerequisites specified in Appendix B to FAR Part 141 (and FAR 61.105) and has the aeronautical knowledge necessary to pass the private pilot knowledge test.

Lesson	Topic	Min. Time in Hours	Pilot Handbook No. of O/L Pgs.	Private Pilot Knowledge Test No. of O/L Pgs.	No. of Questions
	Stage One				
1	Airplanes and Aerodynamics	3.0	54	4	38
2	Airplane Instruments, Engines, and Systems	3.0	62	6	83
3	Airports, Air Traffic Control, and Airspace	3.0	71	10	107
4	Federal Aviation Regulations	3.0	77	16	171
5	Airplane Performance and Weight and Balance	3.0	30	9	61
	Stage One Knowledge Test	1.0			
	Stage Two				
6	Aeromedical Factors and Aeronautical Decision Making	2.0	34	3	30
7	Aviation Weather	3.0	23	4	56
8	Aviation Weather Services	3.0	44	9	73
9	Navigation: Charts, Publications, Flight Computers	3.0	52	15	65
10	Navigation Systems	3.0	36	4	33
11	Cross-Country Flight Planning	3.0	16	7	62
	Stage Two Knowledge Test	1.0			
	End-of-Course Knowledge Test	2.5			

STAGE ONE

Stage One Objective

To develop the student's knowledge of airplanes and the aerodynamic principles of flight. The student will learn about the operation of various airplane systems, airport operations, radio communication procedures, air traffic control (ATC) radar services, and the National Airspace System (NAS). Additionally, the student will become familiar with pertinent Federal Aviation Regulations (FARs) and the accident-reporting requirements of the National Transportation Safety Board (NTSB). Finally, the student will learn how to predict airplane performance and how to control the weight and balance of the airplane.

Stage One Completion Standards

Stage One will have been successfully completed when the student passes the Stage One knowledge test with a minimum passing grade of 80%.

GROUND LESSON 1: AIRPLANES AND AERODYNAMICS

Objective

To develop the student's knowledge of airplanes, the aerodynamics of flight, and airplane stability.

Text References

Pilot Handbook, Study Unit 1, "Airplanes and Aerodynamics" (54 pages)
Private Pilot FAA Knowledge Test, Study Unit 1, "Airplanes and Aerodynamics" (4 pages)

Pilot Handbook Study Unit 1 Contents	No. of Pages	*Private Pilot FAA Knowledge Test* Study Unit 1 Contents	No. of Questions
1.1 Definitions..	5	1.1 Flaps and Rudder................................	3
1.2 The Airplane..	5	1.2 Aerodynamic Forces..........................	4
1.3 Axes of Rotation....................................	1	1.3 Angle of Attack..................................	5
1.4 Flight Controls and Control Surfaces......	5	1.4 Stalls and Spins................................	3
1.5 Forces Acting on the Airplane in Flight...	6	1.5 Frost...	3
1.6 Dynamics of the Airplane in Flight..........	4	1.6 Ground Effect...................................	4
1.7 Ground Effect..	2	1.7 Airplane Turn....................................	1
1.8 How Airplanes Turn...............................	1	1.8 Airplane Stability...............................	6
1.9 Torque (Left-Turning Tendency)..............	4	1.9 Torque and P-Factor.........................	3
1.10 Airplane Stability..................................	7	1.10 Load Factor.....................................	6
1.11 Loads and Load Factors.......................	6		
1.12 Stalls and Spins..................................	7		

Completion Standards

The lesson will have been successfully completed when the student answers the questions in Study Unit 1, "Airplanes and Aerodynamics," of *Private Pilot FAA Knowledge Test, FAA Test Prep Software Download/Test Prep for Windows Mobile,* and/or *Online Ground School* with a minimum passing grade of 80%.

_____

	Dates Studied	Date Completed
Pilot Handbook	____ ____ ____ ____ ____	____
Private Pilot FAA Knowledge Test	____ ____ ____ ____ ____	____

Notes:

GROUND LESSON 2: AIRPLANE INSTRUMENTS, ENGINES, AND SYSTEMS

Objective

To develop the student's knowledge of airplane instruments, engines, and systems.

Text References

Pilot Handbook, Study Unit 2, "Airplane Instruments, Engines, and Systems" (62 pages)
Private Pilot FAA Knowledge Test, Study Unit 2, "Airplane Instruments, Engines, and Systems" (6 pages)

Pilot Handbook Study Unit 2 Contents	No. of Pages	*Private Pilot FAA Knowledge Test* Study Unit 2 Contents	No. of Questions
2.1 Pitot-Static System	2	2.1 Compass Turning Error	8
2.2 Altimeter	3	2.2 Pitot-Static System	4
2.3 Vertical Speed Indicator	1	2.3 Airspeed Indicator	11
2.4 Airspeed Indicator	5	2.4 Altimeter	4
2.5 Gyroscopic Flight Instruments	2	2.5 Types of Altitude	8
2.6 Turn Coordinator	2	2.6 Setting the Altimeter	2
2.7 Turn-and-Slip Indicator	1	2.7 Altimeter Errors	5
2.8 Attitude Indicator	1	2.8 Gyroscopic Instruments	4
2.9 Heading Indicator	2	2.9 Engine Temperature	7
2.10 Magnetic Compass	1	2.10 Constant-Speed Propeller	3
2.11 Compass Errors	4	2.11 Engine Ignition Systems	2
2.12 Glass Cockpit Instrumentation	3	2.12 Carburetor Icing	6
2.13 Airplane Engines	2	2.13 Carburetor Heat	3
2.14 How an Engine Operates	2	2.14 Fuel/Air Mixture	3
2.15 Ignition System	3	2.15 Abnormal Combustion	5
2.16 Induction System	8	2.16 Aviation Fuel Practices	5
2.17 Fuel System	4	2.17 Starting the Engine	2
2.18 Oil System	1	2.18 Electrical System	1
2.19 Cooling System	2		
2.20 Propellers	5		
2.21 Full Authority Digital Engine Control (FADEC)	1		
2.22 Electrical System	4		
2.23 Landing Gear System	3		
2.24 Environmental System	1		
2.25 Deice and Anti-Ice Systems	1		

Completion Standards

The lesson will have been successfully completed when the student answers the questions in Study Unit 2, "Airplane Instruments, Engines, and Systems," of *Private Pilot FAA Knowledge Test*, *FAA Test Prep* Software Download/Test Prep for Windows Mobile, and/or *Online Ground School* with a minimum passing grade of 80%.

	Dates Studied	Date Completed
Pilot Handbook	___ ___ ___ ___ ___	___
Private Pilot FAA Knowledge Test	___ ___ ___ ___ ___	___

Notes:

GROUND LESSON 3: AIRPORTS, AIR TRAFFIC CONTROL, AND AIRSPACE

Objective

To develop the student's knowledge of airports, wake turbulence and collision avoidance, radio communication procedures and phraseology, ATC radar services, and the National Airspace System.

Text References

Pilot Handbook, Study Unit 3, "Airports, Air Traffic Control, and Airspace" (71 pages)
Private Pilot FAA Knowledge Test, Study Unit 3, "Airports, Air Traffic Control, and Airspace" (10 pages)

Pilot Handbook Study Unit 3 Contents	No. of Pages	*Private Pilot FAA Knowledge Test* Study Unit 3 Contents	No. of Questions
3.1 Runway and Taxiway Markings	14	3.1 Runway Markings	6
3.2 Airport Lighting	5	3.2 Taxiway and Destination Signs	6
3.3 Visual Glideslope Indicators	4	3.3 Beacons and Taxiway Lights	6
3.4 Wind and Landing Direction Indicators and Segmented Circles	2	3.4 Airport Traffic Patterns	9
3.5 Airport Traffic Patterns	2	3.5 Visual Approach Slope Indicators (VASI)	11
3.6 Land and Hold Short Operations (LAHSO)	1	3.6 Wake Turbulence	9
3.7 Wake Turbulence	7	3.7 Collision Avoidance	11
3.8 Collision Avoidance	5	3.8 ATIS and Ground Control	4
3.9 Radio Communications and Phraseology	3	3.9 Class D Airspace and Airport Advisory Area	9
3.10 Airports without an Operating Control Tower	3	3.10 Class C Airspace	5
3.11 Automated Weather Reporting Systems	2	3.11 Terminal Radar Programs	3
3.12 Airports with an Operating Control Tower	1	3.12 Transponder Codes	4
3.13 Automatic Terminal Information Service (ATIS)	1	3.13 Radio Phraseology	3
3.14 Ground Control	1	3.14 ATC Traffic Advisories	5
3.15 Tower Control	1	3.15 ATC Light Signals	7
3.16 Approach Control and Departure Control (for VFR Aircraft)	1	3.16 ELTs and VHF/DF	4
3.17 Clearance Delivery	1	3.17 Land and Hold Short Operations (LAHSO)	5
3.18 Emergencies	1		
3.19 Radio Failure Procedures	1		
3.20 Emergency Locator Transmitter (ELT)	2		
3.21 ATC Radar	1		
3.22 Transponder Operation	2		
3.23 Radar Services to VFR Aircraft	3		
3.24 General Dimensions of Airspace	1		
3.25 Controlled and Uncontrolled Airspace	2		
3.26-3.31 Class A, B, C, D, E, and G Airspace	4		
3.32 Special-Use Airspace	1		
3.33 Other Airspace Areas	2		
3.34 Special Flight Rules Areas	2		

Completion Standards

The lesson will have been successfully completed when the student answers the questions in Study Unit 3, "Airports, Air Traffic Control, and Airspace," of *Private Pilot FAA Knowledge Test*, *FAA Test Prep* Software Download/Test Prep for Windows Mobile, and/or *Online Ground School* with a minimum passing grade of 80%.

	Dates Studied	Date Completed
Pilot Handbook	____ ____ ____ ____ ____	____
Private Pilot FAA Knowledge Test	____ ____ ____ ____ ____	____

Notes:

GROUND LESSON 4: FEDERAL AVIATION REGULATIONS

Objective

To develop the student's knowledge of pertinent Federal Aviation Regulations (FARs) and the accident-reporting rules of the National Transportation Safety Board (NTSB).

Text References

Pilot Handbook, Study Unit 4, "Federal Aviation Regulations" (77 pages)
Private Pilot FAA Knowledge Test, Study Unit 4, "Federal Aviation Regulations" (except Subunit 4.6, "Recreational Pilot Related FARs") (16 pages)

Pilot Handbook Study Unit 4 Contents	No. of Pages	*Private Pilot FAA Knowledge Test* Study Unit 4 Contents	No. of Questions
4.1 Federal Aviation Regulations	1	4.1 FAR Part 1	13
4.2 Part 1 -- Definitions and Abbreviations	4	4.2 FAR Part 21	1
4.3 Part 21 -- Certification Procedures for Products and Parts	1	4.3 FAR Part 39	2
4.4 Part 39 -- Airworthiness Directives	1	4.4 FAR Part 43	5
4.5 Part 43 -- Maintenance, Preventive Maintenance, Rebuilding, and Alteration	1	4.5 FAR Part 61	31
4.6 Part 61 -- Certification: Pilots, Flight Instructors, and Ground Instructors	30	4.6 Recreational Pilot Related FARs	NA
4.7 Part 67 -- Medical Standards and Certification	4	4.7 FAR Part 71	2
4.8 Part 91 -- General Operating and Flight Rules	26	4.8 FAR Part 91: 91.3 - 91.151	50
4.9 NTSB Part 830 -- Notification and Reporting of Aircraft Accidents or Incidents and Overdue Aircraft, and Preservation of Aircraft Wreckage, Mail, Cargo, and Records	2	4.9 FAR Part 91: 91.155 - 91.519	60
4.10 Summary of Current FAR Part Numbers	7	4.10 NTSB Part 830	7

Completion Standards

The lesson will have been successfully completed when the student answers the questions in Study Unit 4, "Federal Aviation Regulations," of *Private Pilot FAA Knowledge Test, FAA Test Prep* Software Download/Test Prep for Windows Mobile, and *Online Ground School* with a minimum passing grade of 80%.

	Dates Studied	Date Completed
Pilot Handbook	____ ____ ____ ____ ____	____
Private Pilot FAA Knowledge Test	____ ____ ____ ____ ____	____

Notes:

GROUND LESSON 5: AIRPLANE PERFORMANCE AND WEIGHT AND BALANCE

Objective

To develop the student's ability to determine airplane performance, including weight and balance. Additionally, the student will learn the adverse effects of exceeding the airplane's limitations.

Text References

Pilot Handbook, Study Unit 5, "Airplane Performance and Weight and Balance" (30 pages)
Private Pilot FAA Knowledge Test, Study Unit 5, "Airplane Performance and Weight and Balance" (9 pages)

Pilot Handbook Study Unit 5 Contents	No. of Pages	*Private Pilot FAA Knowledge Test* Study Unit 5 Contents	No. of Questions
5.1 Determinants of Airplane Performance	2	5.1 Density Altitude	8
5.2 Standard Atmosphere	1	5.2 Density Altitude Computations	8
5.3 Pressure Altitude	1	5.3 Takeoff Distance	4
5.4 Density Altitude	3	5.4 Cruise Power Settings	5
5.5 Takeoff Performance	2	5.5 Crosswind Components	6
5.6 Climb Performance	3	5.6 Landing Distance	11
5.7 Cruise and Range Performance	1	5.7 Weight and Balance Definitions	5
5.8 Glide Performance	1	5.8 Center of Gravity Calculations	2
5.9 Crosswind Performance	1	5.8 Center of Gravity Graphs	4
5.10 Landing Performance	3	5.10 Center of Gravity Tables	8
5.11 Weight and Balance Overview	2		
5.12 Weight and Balance Terms	1		
5.13 Basic Principles of Weight and Balance	1		
5.14 Methods of Determining Weight and Balance	1		
5.15 Center of Gravity Calculations	1		
5.16 Center of Gravity Charts	3		
5.17 Center of Gravity Tables	2		
5.18 Weight Change and Weight Shift Computations	1		

Completion Standards

The lesson will have been successfully completed when the student answers the questions in Study Unit 5, "Airplane Performance and Weight and Balance," of *Private Pilot FAA Knowledge Test*, *FAA Test Prep* Software Download/Test Prep for Windows Mobile, and/or *Online Ground School* with a minimum passing grade of 80%.

	Dates Studied	Date Completed
Pilot Handbook	____ ____ ____ ____ ____	____
Private Pilot FAA Knowledge Test	____ ____ ____ ____ ____	____

Notes:

STAGE ONE KNOWLEDGE TEST

Objective

To evaluate the student's understanding of the material presented during Ground Lesson 1 through Ground Lesson 5. The Stage One knowledge test consists of 25 questions on pages 62 and 63.

Content

Lesson
1   Airplanes and Aerodynamics
2   Airplane Instruments, Engines, and Systems
3   Airports, Air Traffic Control, and Airspace
4   Federal Aviation Regulations
5   Airplane Performance and Weight and Balance

Completion Standards

The lesson will have been successfully completed when the student has completed the Stage One knowledge test with a minimum passing grade of 80%.

STAGE TWO

Stage Two Objective

To develop the student's knowledge of medical factors and the aeronautical decision-making process related to all flights. The student will learn how weather affects flying. The student will learn how to obtain weather briefings and how to interpret aviation reports, forecasts, and charts. Additionally, the student will learn how to use navigation charts, plotters, flight computers, and flight publications for cross-country flight planning. Finally, the student will learn how to use various navigation systems.

Stage Two Completion Standards

Stage Two will have been successfully completed when the student passes the Stage Two knowledge test with a minimum passing grade of 80%.

Lesson	Topic	Min. Time
6	Aeromedical Factors and Aeronautical Decision Making	2.0
7	Aviation Weather	3.0
8	Aviation Weather Services	3.0
9	Navigation: Charts, Publications, Flight Computers	3.0
10	Navigation Systems	3.0
11	Cross-Country Flight Planning	3.0
	Stage Two Knowledge Test	1.0
	End-of-Course Knowledge Test	2.5

GROUND LESSON 6: AEROMEDICAL FACTORS AND AERONAUTICAL DECISION MAKING

Objective

To develop the student's knowledge of the medical factors related to flight and to the aeronautical decision making (ADM) process.

Text References

Pilot Handbook, Study Unit 6, "Aeromedical Factors and Aeronautical Decision Making (ADM)" (34 pages)

Private Pilot FAA Knowledge Test, Study Unit 6, "Aeromedical Factors and Aeronautical Decision Making (ADM)" (3 pages)

Pilot Handbook Study Unit 6 Contents	No. of Pages	*Private Pilot FAA Knowledge Test* Study Unit 6 Contents	No. of Questions
6.1 Fitness for Flight	4	6.1 Hypoxia	1
6.2 Hypoxia	2	6.2 Hyperventilation	4
6.3 Dehydration	1	6.3 Spatial Disorientation	5
6.4 Hyperventilation	1	6.4 Vision	5
6.5 Carbon Monoxide Poisoning	2	6.5 Carbon Monoxide	2
6.6 Decompression Sickness after Scuba Diving	1	6.6 Aeronautical Decision Making (ADM)	13
6.7 Motion Sickness	1		
6.8 Sinus and Ear Block	1		
6.9 Spatial Disorientation	1		
6.10 Illusions in Flight	2		
6.11 Vision	3		
6.12 Aeronautical Decision Making (ADM)	7		
6.13 Weather-Related Decision Making	2		
6.14 Stress and Flying	3		
6.15 Identifying the Enemy	2		
6.16 Crew Resource Management (CRM)	3		

Completion Standards

The lesson will have been successfully completed when the student answers the questions in Study Unit 6, "Aeromedical Factors and Aeronautical Decision Making (ADM)," of *Private Pilot FAA Knowledge Test*, *FAA Test Prep* Software Download/Test Prep for Windows Mobile, and/or *Online Ground School* with a minimum passing grade of 80%.

_____

	Dates Studied	Date Completed
Pilot Handbook	____ ____ ____ ____ ____	____
Private Pilot FAA Knowledge Test	____ ____ ____ ____ ____	____

Notes:

GROUND LESSON 7: AVIATION WEATHER

Objective

To develop the student's knowledge of the fundamentals of weather, as associated with the operation of an airplane.

Text References

Pilot Handbook, Study Unit 7, "Aviation Weather" (23 pages)
Private Pilot FAA Knowledge Test, Study Unit 7, "Aviation Weather" (4 pages)

Pilot Handbook Study Unit 7 Contents	No. of Pages	*Private Pilot FAA Knowledge Test* Study Unit 7 Contents	No. of Questions
7.1 The Earth's Atmosphere	2	7.1 Causes of Weather	3
7.2 Temperature	1	7.2 Convective Currents	2
7.3 Atmospheric Pressure	4	7.3 Fronts	3
7.4 Wind	2	7.4 Thunderstorms	9
7.5 Moisture, Cloud Formation, and Precipitation	2	7.5 Icing	3
7.6 Stable and Unstable Air	1	7.6 Mountain Wave	3
7.7 Clouds	1	7.7 Wind Shear	3
7.8 Air Masses and Fronts	2	7.8 Temperature/Dew Point and Fog	10
7.9 Turbulence	3	7.9 Clouds	7
7.10 Icing	2	7.10 Stability of Air Masses	9
7.11 Thunderstorms	1	7.11 Temperature Inversions	4
7.12 Fog	1		

Completion Standards

The lesson will have been successfully completed when the student answers the questions in Study Unit 7, "Aviation Weather," of *Private Pilot FAA Knowledge Test*, *FAA Test Prep* Software Download/Test Prep for Windows Mobile, and/or *Online Ground School* with a minimum passing grade of 80%.

	Dates Studied	Date Completed
Pilot Handbook	____ ____ ____ ____ ____	____
Private Pilot FAA Knowledge Test	____ ____ ____ ____ ____	____

Notes:

GROUND LESSON 8: AVIATION WEATHER SERVICES

Objective

To develop the student's ability to interpret and use weather charts, reports, forecasts, and broadcasts; and to develop the student's knowledge of the procedure to obtain weather briefings.

Text References

Pilot Handbook, Study Unit 8, "Aviation Weather Services" (44 pages)
Private Pilot FAA Knowledge Test, Study Unit 8, "Aviation Weather Services" (9 pages)

Pilot Handbook Study Unit 8 Contents	No. of Pages	*Private Pilot FAA Knowledge Test* Study Unit 8 Contents	No. of Questions
8.1 Flight Service Station (FSS)	3	8.1 Weather Briefings	10
8.2 Aviation Routine Weather Report (METAR)	7	8.2 Aviation Routine Weather Report (METAR)	6
8.3 Pilot Weather Report (PIREP)	1	8.3 Pilot Weather Report (PIREP)	5
8.4 Terminal Aerodrome Forecast (TAF)	4	8.4 Aviation Area Forecast	8
8.5 Aviation Area Forecast (FA)	3	8.5 Terminal Aerodrome Forecast (TAF)	8
8.6 In-Flight Aviation Weather Advisories	4	8.6 Weather Depiction Charts	6
8.7 Winds and Temperatures Aloft Forecast (FB)	1	8.7 Radar Summary Charts and Radar Weather	
8.8 Surface Analysis Chart	1	Reports	7
8.9 Weather Depiction Chart	2	8.8 En Route Flight Advisory Service (EFAS)	3
8.10 Radar Summary Chart	2	8.9 Winds and Temperatures Aloft Forecasts	
8.11 Short-Range Surface Prognostic (PROG)		(FB)	7
Chart	3	8.10 Significant Weather Prognostic Charts	5
8.12 Low-Level Significant Weather (SIGWX) Chart	2	8.11 Transcribed Weather Broadcasts	3
8.13 DUATS	8	8.12 AIRMETs and SIGMETs	5
8.14 Aviation Weather Resources on the Internet	4		

Completion Standards

The lesson will have been successfully completed when the student answers the questions in Study Unit 8, "Aviation Weather Services," of *Private Pilot FAA Knowledge Test*, *FAA Test Prep* Software Download/Test Prep for Windows Mobile, and/or *Online Ground School* with a minimum passing grade of 80%.

	Dates Studied	Date Completed
Pilot Handbook	____ ____ ____ ____ ____	____
Private Pilot FAA Knowledge Test	____ ____ ____ ____ ____	____

Notes:

GROUND LESSON 9: NAVIGATION: CHARTS, PUBLICATIONS, FLIGHT COMPUTERS

Objective

To develop the student's knowledge of, and the ability to use, navigation charts, publications, and a flight computer in planning a VFR cross-country flight.

Text References

Pilot Handbook, Study Unit 9, "Navigation: Charts, Publications, Flight Computers" (52 pages)
Private Pilot FAA Knowledge Test, Study Unit 9, "Navigation: Charts and Publications" (15 pages)

Pilot Handbook Study Unit 9 Contents	No. of Pages	*Private Pilot FAA Knowledge Test* Study Unit 9 Contents	No. of Questions
9.1 VFR Navigation Charts................................	2	9.1 Longitude and Latitude...........................	6
9.2 Longitude and Latitude.............................	3	9.2 Airspace and Altitudes...........................	33
9.3 Sectional Chart Symbology......................	8	9.3 Identifying Landmarks............................	4
9.4 FAA Advisory Circulars (AC)....................	2	9.4 Radio Frequencies.................................	12
9.5 Aeronautical Information Manual (AIM)......	1	9.5 FAA Advisory Circulars..........................	4
9.6 Airport/Facility Directory (A/FD)...............	2	9.6 Airport/Facility Directory.........................	5
9.7 Notice to Airmen (NOTAM) System.........	4	9.7 Notices to Airmen Publication (NTAP)................	1
9.8 Flight Computers...................................	1		
9.9 The Gleim Flight Computer......................	1		
9.10 The Calculator Side of the Flight Computer..........	1		
9.11 Conversion of Nautical Miles to Statute Miles and Vice Versa......................	1		
9.12 Speed, Distance, and Time Computations...........	4		
9.13 Fuel Computations................................	3		
9.14 True Airspeed and Density Altitude......................	2		
9.15 Corrected (Approximately True) Altitude..............	1		
9.16 Off-Course Correction...........................	1		
9.17 Radius of Action..................................	1		
9.18 Other Conversions...............................	2		
9.19 Temperature Conversions......................	1		
9.20 The Wind Side of Gleim's Flight Computer...........	1		
9.21 Determining Magnetic Heading and Groundspeed......................	2		
9.22 Determining Wind Direction and Speed................	1		
9.23 Determining Altitude for Most Favorable Winds....	1		
9.24 Alternative: E6-B Computer Approach to Magnetic Heading..............................	1		
9.25 Information Side of Sliding Card (Gleim E6B).......	2		
9.26-9.28 Electronic Flight Computers, ASA CX-2, and Sporty's E6B......................	4		

Completion Standards

The lesson will have been successfully completed when the student answers the questions in Study Unit 9, "Navigation: Charts and Publications," of *Private Pilot FAA Knowledge Test*, *FAA Test Prep* Software Download/Test Prep for Windows Mobile, and/or *Online Ground School* with a minimum passing grade of 80%.

	Dates Studied	Date Completed
Pilot Handbook	____ ____ ____ ____ ____	____
Private Pilot FAA Knowledge Test	____ ____ ____ ____ ____	____

Notes:

GROUND LESSON 10: NAVIGATION SYSTEMS

Objective

To develop the student's knowledge of various navigation systems.

Text References

Pilot Handbook, Study Unit 10, "Navigation Systems" (36 pages)
Private Pilot FAA Knowledge Test, Study Unit 10, "Navigation Systems" (4 pages)

Pilot Handbook Study Unit 10 Contents	No. of Pages	*Private Pilot FAA Knowledge Test* Study Unit 10 Contents	No. of Questions
10.1 Basic Radio Principles	5	10.1 VOR Test Facility (VOT)	1
10.2 VHF Omnidirectional Range (VOR)	12	10.2 Determining Position	11
10.3 Distance-Measuring Equipment (DME)	1	10.3 Automatic Direction Finder (ADF)	18
10.4 Automatic Direction Finder (ADF)	7	10.4 Global Positioning System (GPS)	3
10.5 Area Navigation (RNAV)	1		
10.6 VORTAC-Based RNAV	1		
10.7 Long-Range Navigation (LORAN)	3		
10.8 Global Positioning System (GPS)	6		

Completion Standards

The lesson will have been successfully completed when the student answers the questions in Study Unit 10, "Navigation Systems," of *Private Pilot FAA Knowledge Test*, *FAA Test Prep* Software Download/Test Prep for Windows Mobile, and/or *Online Ground School* with a minimum passing grade of 80%.

	Dates Studied					Date Completed
Pilot Handbook	____	____	____	____	____	____
Private Pilot FAA Knowledge Test	____	____	____	____	____	____

Notes:

GROUND LESSON 11: CROSS-COUNTRY FLIGHT PLANNING

Objective

To further develop the student's ability to properly plan a VFR cross-country flight. Additionally, the student is introduced to the procedures to use when lost and when diverting to an alternate airport.

Text References

Pilot Handbook, Study Unit 11, "Cross-Country Flight Planning" (except Subunit 11.7, "IFR Cross-Country Procedures") (16 pages)
Private Pilot FAA Knowledge Test, Study Unit 11, "Cross-Country Flight Planning" (7 pages)

Pilot Handbook Study Unit 11 Contents	No. of Pages	Private Pilot FAA Knowledge Test Study Unit 11 Contents	No. of Questions
11.1 Preflight Preparation	7	11.1 VFR Flight Plan	7
11.2 VFR Flight Plan	2	11.2 Preflight Inspection	3
11.3 Weight and Balance	1	11.3 Miscellaneous Airspeed Questions	4
11.4 Navigation	1	11.4 Taxiing Technique	7
11.5 Diversion to an Alternate Airport	2	11.5 Magnetic Course	7
11.6 Lost Procedures	3	11.6 Magnetic Heading	9
11.7 IFR Cross-Country Procedures	NA	11.7 Compass Heading	1
		11.8 Time En Route	13
		11.9 Time Zone Corrections	6
		11.10 Fundamentals of Flight	1
		11.11 Rectangular Course	2
		11.12 S-Turns Across a Road	1
		11.13 Landings	1

Completion Standards

The lesson will have been successfully completed when the student answers the questions in Study Unit 11, "Cross-Country Flight Planning," of *Private Pilot FAA Knowledge Test*, *FAA Test Prep* Software Download/Test Prep for Windows Mobile, and/or *Online Ground School* with a minimum passing grade of 80%.

	Dates Studied	Date Completed
Pilot Handbook	____ ____ ____ ____ ____	____
Private Pilot FAA Knowledge Test	____ ____ ____ ____ ____	____

Notes:

STAGE TWO KNOWLEDGE TEST

Objective

To evaluate the student's understanding of the material presented during Ground Lesson 6 through Ground Lesson 11. The Stage Two knowledge test consists of 25 questions on pages 64 and 65.

Content

<u>Lesson</u> (Lessons 1-5 were Stage One.)
- 6   Aeromedical Factors and Aeronautical Decision Making
- 7   Aviation Weather
- 8   Aviation Weather Services
- 9   Navigation: Charts, Publications, Flight Publications
- 10   Navigation Systems
- 11   Cross-Country Flight Planning

Completion Standards

The lesson will have been successfully completed when the student has completed the Stage Two knowledge test with a minimum passing grade of 80%.

END-OF-COURSE KNOWLEDGE TEST

Objective

To evaluate the student's comprehension of the material covered in the ground training course and to determine the student's readiness to take the FAA private pilot knowledge test. The end-of-course knowledge test consists of 60 questions on pages 66 through 70.

Content

Practice Private Pilot Knowledge Test

Completion Standards

The lesson will have been successfully completed when the student has completed the practice private pilot knowledge test with a minimum passing grade of 80%.

PRIVATE PILOT
FLIGHT TRAINING SYLLABUS –
AIRPLANE SINGLE-ENGINE LAND

FLIGHT TRAINING COURSE OBJECTIVES

The student will obtain the aeronautical knowledge and experience and demonstrate the flight proficiency necessary to meet the requirements for a private pilot certificate with an airplane category rating and single-engine land class rating.

FLIGHT TRAINING COURSE COMPLETION STANDARDS

The student will demonstrate through the stage checks and school records that (s)he has the necessary flight proficiency and aeronautical experience to obtain a private pilot certificate with an airplane category rating and single-engine land class rating.

Lesson	Topic	Number of Pages in Reading Assignment
	Stage One	
1	Introduction to Flight	70
2	Four Fundamentals of Flight	63
3	Basic Instrument Maneuvers	21
4	Slow Flight and Stalls	27
5	Emergency Operations	34
6	Steep Turns and Ground Reference Maneuvers	33
7	Review	*
8	Go-Around and Forward Slip to a Landing	13
9	Presolo Review	*
10	Presolo Review	*
11	First Solo	45
12	Stage One Check	*
		306
	Stage Two	
13	Second Solo	*
14	Short-Field and Soft-Field Takeoffs and Landings	22
15	Solo Maneuvers Review	*
16	Navigation Systems	55
17	Dual Cross-Country	199
18	Night Flight -- Local	134
19	Night Cross-Country	2
20	Solo Cross-Country	*
20A	Solo Cross-Country (Part 61)	*
20B	Solo Cross-Country (Part 61)	*
21	Maneuvers Review	*
22	Solo Practice	*
23	Maneuvers Review	*
24	Solo Practice	*
25	Stage Two Check	*
		412

*Reading assignment consists of review only, no new materials.

The following is a brief description of the parts of each flight lesson in this syllabus:

Objective: We open each lesson with an objective, usually a sentence or two, to help you gain perspective and understand the goal for that particular lesson.

Text References: This section tells you which reference books you will need to study or refer to while mastering the tasks within the lesson. Abbreviations are given to facilitate the cross-referencing process.

Content: Each lesson contains a list of the tasks required to be completed before moving to the next lesson. A task may be listed as a "review item" (a task that was covered in a previous lesson) or as a "new item" (a task which is introduced to you for the first time). Each task is preceded by three blank "checkoff" boxes, which may be used by your CFI to keep track of your progress and to indicate that each task was completed.

There are three boxes because it may take more than one flight to complete the lesson. Your CFI may mark the box(es) next to each task in one of the following methods (or any other method desired):

√ - task completed to lesson completion standards	D - demonstrated by instructor * A - accomplished by you S - safe/satisfactory P - meets PTS standards	1 - above lesson standard 2 - meets lesson standard 3 - below lesson standard

Most tasks are followed by book and page references that tell you where to find the information you need to study to accomplish the task successfully.

The last task in each flight lesson is labeled "Additional items at CFI's discretion," and is followed by several blank lines. This area can be used to record any extra items that your CFI feels are appropriate to the lesson, taking into account such variables as weather, local operational considerations, and your progress as a student.

NOTE: CFIs are reminded not to limit themselves to the blank lines provided–use as much of the page as you need.

Completion Standards: Based on these standards, your CFI determines how well you have met the objective of the lesson in terms of knowledge and skill.

Instructor's Comments and Lesson Assignment: Space is provided for your CFI's critique of the lesson, which you can refer to later. Your instructor may also write any specific assignment for the next lesson.

Reading Assignments for Flight Lessons

You are expected to be prepared for each flight lesson. Our reading assignments will help you understand what is going to happen and how and why you need to do everything BEFORE you go to the airport.

Each flight lesson in this book contains

- Objective
- Text references
- Content
    - √ Review items
    - √ New items
- Completion standards
- Comments and student/instructor signoffs

Next to each item in the Content section, we have provided the page number(s) to read in *Private Pilot Flight Maneuvers and Practical Test Prep* (FM) and/or *Pilot Handbook* (PH), and the section to read, if appropriate, in your airplane's Pilot's Operating Handbook (POH).

For the new items, you should read the material and attempt to understand the basic concepts. Try to anticipate and visualize the concepts and flight maneuvers. With this basic knowledge, your CFI can expand on the specific and finer points, especially when explaining how a task is done in your specific airplane.

After your flight lesson, task items are fresh in your mind; they will make sense, and you should be able to understand and learn more.

Study review items so you can explain them to your CFI and your examiner.

After you study, relax and plan a time to begin reading to prepare for the next flight lesson.

STAGE ONE

Stage One Objective

The student will obtain the basic flying procedures and skills necessary for the first solo flight.

Stage One Completion Standards

The stage will be completed when the student satisfactorily passes the Stage One check and is able to conduct solo flights safely.

Lesson	Topic
	Stage One
1	Introduction to Flight
2	Four Fundamentals of Flight
3	Basic Instrument Maneuvers
4	Slow Flight and Stalls
5	Emergency Operations
6	Steep Turns and Ground Reference Maneuvers
7	Review
8	Go-Around and Forward Slip to a Landing
9	Presolo Review
10	Presolo Review
11	First Solo
12	Stage One Check

FLIGHT LESSON 1: INTRODUCTION TO FLIGHT

Objective

To familiarize the student with the training airplane, its operating characteristics, cockpit controls, and the instruments and systems. The student will be introduced to preflight and postflight procedures, the use of checklists, and the safety precautions to be followed. Additionally, the student will be introduced to the effect and use of the flight controls and the local practice area and airport.

Text References

Private Pilot Flight Maneuvers and Practical Test Prep (FM)
Pilot Handbook (PH)
Pilot's Operating Handbook (POH)

Content

1.   Preflight briefing
2.   New items

☐☐☐ Certificates and documents - FM 41-44
    ☐☐☐ Airplane logbooks - CFI
    ☐☐☐ Airworthiness requirements -
         FM 45-49
☐☐☐ Use of checklists - FM 81; POH-4
☐☐☐ Preflight inspection - FM 78-82; POH-4
    ☐☐☐ Airplane servicing - CFI
☐☐☐ Location of emergency equipment and
     survival gear - CFI
☐☐☐ Airplane systems - POH-7; CFI
☐☐☐ Engine starting - FM 86-89; POH-4
☐☐☐ Taxiing - FM 90-94; POH-4
☐☐☐ Before-takeoff check - FM 95-98; POH-4
☐☐☐ Normal and crosswind takeoff and climb -
     FM 110-117; POH-4

☐☐☐ Effect and use of primary flight controls
     and trim - PH 36-39
☐☐☐ Practice area familiarization - CFI
☐☐☐ Collision avoidance procedures - PH 176-181
☐☐☐ Normal and crosswind approach -
     FM 118-134; POH-4
☐☐☐ After-landing procedures - FM 284; POH-4
☐☐☐ Parking and securing the airplane -
     FM 285-288; POH-4
☐☐☐ Additional items at CFI's discretion _____
_____
_____

3.   Postflight critique and preview of next lesson

Completion Standards

The lesson will have been successfully completed when the student displays an understanding of the airplane's systems, the use of checklists, preflight procedures, and postflight procedures. Additionally, the student will be familiar with the correct use of the controls, the local practice area, and the airport.

Instructor's comments:_____

_____

Lesson assignment:_____

_____

Notes:_____

_____

_____

_____

_____

FLIGHT LESSON 2: FOUR FUNDAMENTALS OF FLIGHT

Objective

To develop the student's skill in the performance of the four basic flight maneuvers (straight-and-level, turns, climbs, and descents). Additionally, the student will be introduced to radio communication procedures, airport markings, and traffic patterns.

Text References

Private Pilot Flight Maneuvers and Practical Test Prep (FM)
Pilot Handbook (PH)
Pilot's Operating Handbook (POH)

Content

1. Flight Lesson 1 complete? Yes ___   Copy of lesson placed in student's folder? Yes ___
2. Preflight briefing
3. Review items
   - ☐☐☐ Use of checklists - FM 81; POH-4
   - ☐☐☐ Certificates and documents - FM 41-44
   - ☐☐☐ Preflight inspection - FM 78-82; POH-4
   - ☐☐☐ Engine starting - FM 86-89; POH-4
   - ☐☐☐ Taxiing - FM 90-94; POH-4
   - ☐☐☐ Before-takeoff check - FM 95-98; POH-4

   - ☐☐☐ Normal and crosswind takeoff and climb - FM 110-117; POH-4
   - ☐☐☐ Collision avoidance procedures - PH 176-181
   - ☐☐☐ Normal and crosswind approach - FM 118-134; POH-4
   - ☐☐☐ Postflight procedures - FM 284-288; POH-4

4. New items
   - ☐☐☐ Cockpit management - FM 83-85
   - ☐☐☐ Radio communication procedures - FM 99-102; PH 181-184
   - ☐☐☐ Airport and runway markings - PH 142-155
   - ☐☐☐ Traffic patterns - FM 103-106; PH 166-168
   - ☐☐☐ Straight-and-level flight - FM 21-22
   - ☐☐☐ Climbs and climbing turns - FM 24-26; POH-4
       - ☐☐☐ Cruise climb
       - ☐☐☐ Best rate of climb
       - ☐☐☐ Best angle of climb

   - ☐☐☐ Turns to headings - FM 22-24
   - ☐☐☐ Descents and descending turns - FM 26; POH-4
       - ☐☐☐ Cruise descent
       - ☐☐☐ Traffic pattern descent
       - ☐☐☐ Power-off glide
   - ☐☐☐ Level-off from climbs and descents - FM 25-26
   - ☐☐☐ Torque effects - PH 54-58
   - ☐☐☐ Additional items at CFI's discretion _____

5. Postflight critique and preview of next lesson

Completion Standards

The lesson will have been successfully completed when the student can, with instructor assistance, conduct a preflight inspection, properly use checklists, taxi, perform a before-takeoff check, and make a normal and crosswind takeoff. Additionally, the student will display an understanding of the four fundamentals of flight and the various climb and descent attitudes.

Instructor's comments:_____

_____

Lesson assignment:_____

_____

Notes:_____

_____

_____

_____

FLIGHT LESSON 3: BASIC INSTRUMENT MANEUVERS

Objective

To improve the student's proficiency in the four fundamentals of flight and to introduce the student to basic instrument maneuvers.

Text References

Private Pilot Flight Maneuvers and Practical Test Prep (FM)
Pilot Handbook (PH)

Content

1. Flight Lesson 2 complete? Yes ___   Copy of lesson placed in student's folder? Yes ___
2. Preflight briefing
3. Review items

    ☐☐☐ Use of checklists - FM 81
    ☐☐☐ Radio communication procedures -
          FM 99-102; PH 181-184
    ☐☐☐ Certificates and documents - FM 41-45
    ☐☐☐ Preflight inspection - FM 78-82
    ☐☐☐ Engine starting - FM 86-89
    ☐☐☐ Taxiing - FM 90-94
    ☐☐☐ Before-takeoff check - FM 95-88
    ☐☐☐ Normal and crosswind takeoff and climb -
          FM 110-117

    ☐☐☐ Straight-and-level flight - FM 21-22
    ☐☐☐ Climbs - FM 24-26
    ☐☐☐ Descents - FM 26
    ☐☐☐ Turns to a heading - FM 22-24
    ☐☐☐ Collision avoidance procedures - PH 176-181
    ☐☐☐ Traffic patterns - FM 103-106; PH 166-168
    ☐☐☐ Normal and crosswind approach - FM 118-134
    ☐☐☐ Postflight procedures - FM 284-287

4. New items

    ☐☐☐ Taxiing in a crosswind - FM 91-92
    ☐☐☐ Attitude instrument flying - FM 225-227
    ☐☐☐ Straight-and-level flight (IR)* - FM 228-231
    ☐☐☐ Constant airspeed climbs (IR) -
          FM 232-235

    ☐☐☐ Constant airspeed descents (IR) - FM 236-240
    ☐☐☐ Turns to a heading (IR) - FM 241-243
    ☐☐☐ Additional items at CFI's discretion _____

    * IR means instrument references only, which can be taught by CFIs in contrast to IFR training by CFIIs.

5. Postflight critique and preview of next lesson

Completion Standards

The lesson will have been successfully completed when the student demonstrates an increased understanding of the four fundamentals of flight by use of proper controls. The student will, with instructor assistance, become more proficient in the preflight procedures and a normal crosswind takeoff. Additionally, the student will display an understanding of the basic instrument maneuvers.

Instructor's comments:_____

_____

Lesson assignment:_____

_____

Notes:_____

_____

_____

_____

_____

FLIGHT LESSON 4: SLOW FLIGHT AND STALLS

Objective

To improve the student's proficiency in the performance of the four fundamentals of flight and to introduce maneuvering during slow flight, stalls, and spin awareness.

Text References

Private Pilot Flight Maneuvers and Practical Test Prep (FM)
Pilot Handbook (PH)
Pilot's Operating Handbook (POH)

Content

1. Flight Lesson 3 complete? Yes ___   Copy of lesson placed in student's folder? Yes ___
2. Preflight briefing
3. Review items
    - ☐☐☐ Use of checklists - FM 81; POH-4
    - ☐☐☐ Airplane systems - FM 68-71; PH 79-140; POH-7
    - ☐☐☐ Preflight inspection - FM 78-82
    - ☐☐☐ Collision avoidance procedures - PH 176-181
    - ☐☐☐ Engine starting - FM 86-89
    - ☐☐☐ Radio communication procedures - FM 99-102; PH 181-184
    - ☐☐☐ Airport and runway markings - PH 142-155

    - ☐☐☐ Taxiing - FM 90-94
    - ☐☐☐ Before-takeoff check - FM 95-98
    - ☐☐☐ Normal and crosswind takeoff and climb - FM 110-117
    - ☐☐☐ Four fundamentals of flight - FM 19-26
    - ☐☐☐ Traffic patterns - FM 103-106; PH 166-168
    - ☐☐☐ Normal and crosswind approach - FM 118-134
    - ☐☐☐ Postflight procedures - FM 284-287

4. New items
    - ☐☐☐ Maneuvering during slow flight - FM 206-210; PH 50-51
    - ☐☐☐ Power-off stalls (entered from straight flight) - FM 211-215; PH 72-76
    - ☐☐☐ Power-on stalls (entered from straight flight) - FM 216-220; PH 72-76
    - ☐☐☐ Spin awareness - FM 221-222; PH 77-78; POH-3
    - ☐☐☐ Additional items at CFI's discretion _____

5. Postflight critique and preview of next lesson

Completion Standards

The lesson will have been successfully completed when the student displays proficiency in the four fundamentals of flight by maintaining altitude, ±250 ft.; airspeed, ±20 kt.; and heading, ±20°. During this and subsequent flight lessons, the student should be proficient in the preflight inspection, engine starting, taxiing, the before-takeoff check, and the postflight procedures without instructor assistance. The student should perform normal and crosswind takeoffs without instructor assistance. The student will show an increase in proficiency in traffic patterns and approaches with the instructor still performing the landing. Finally, the student will display an understanding of maneuvering during slow flight, the indications of an approaching stall, the proper recovery procedures, and the conditions necessary for a spin to occur.

Instructor's comments:_____

_____

Lesson assignment:_____

_____

Notes:_____

_____

FLIGHT LESSON 5: EMERGENCY OPERATIONS

Objective

To improve the student's proficiency while maneuvering during slow flight and the recognition of and correct recovery from stalls. Additionally, the student will be introduced to emergency operations and normal landings.

Text References

Private Pilot Flight Maneuvers and Practical Test Prep (FM)
Pilot Handbook (PH)
Pilot's Operating Handbook (POH)

Content

1. Flight Lesson 4 complete? Yes ___   Copy of lesson placed in student's folder? Yes ___
2. Preflight briefing
3. Review items
    - ☐☐☐ Maneuvering during slow flight - FM 206-210; PH 50-51
    - ☐☐☐ Power-off stall (entered from straight flight) - FM 211-215; PH 72-76
    - ☐☐☐ Power-on stall (entered from straight flight) - FM 216-220; PH 72-76
    - ☐☐☐ Spin awareness - FM 221-222; PH 77-78; POH-3
    - ☐☐☐ Normal and crosswind takeoff and approach - FM 118-134

4. New items
    - ☐☐☐ Emergency descent - FM 255-256; POH-3
    - ☐☐☐ Emergency approach and landing - FM 257-263; POH-3
    - ☐☐☐ Systems and equipment malfunctions - FM 264-265; POH-3
    - ☐☐☐ Emergency equipment and survival gear - FM 266-267
    - ☐☐☐ Emergencies during takeoff roll, initial climb, cruise, descent, and in the traffic pattern - FM 257-263; POH-3
    - ☐☐☐ Normal and crosswind landing - FM 118-134
    - ☐☐☐ Recovery from bouncing and ballooning during landing - FM 129-131
    - ☐☐☐ Additional items at CFI's discretion _____

5. Postflight critique and preview of next lesson

Completion Standards

The lesson will have been successfully completed when the student displays an understanding of the procedures to be used during various emergency operations and should be able to make a normal landing with instructor assistance. Additionally, the student will demonstrate improved proficiency in maneuvering during slow flight and improved recognition of and recovery from stalls. The student should be able to maintain altitude, ±200 ft.; airspeed, ±15 kt.; and heading, ±20° during straight-and-level flight.

Instructor's comments:_____

_____

Lesson assignment:_____

_____

Notes:_____

_____

_____

_____

_____

FLIGHT LESSON 6: STEEP TURNS AND GROUND REFERENCE MANEUVERS

Objective

To review previous lessons to gain proficiency and to introduce the student to steep turns and ground reference maneuvers.

Text References

Private Pilot Flight Maneuvers and Practical Test Prep (FM)
Pilot Handbook (PH)
Pilot's Operating Handbook (POH)

Content

1. Flight Lesson 5 complete? Yes ___   Copy of lesson placed in student's folder? Yes ___
2. Preflight briefing
3. Review items
    - □□□ Normal and crosswind takeoff and landing - FM 118-134
    - □□□ Emergency descent - FM 255-256; POH-3
    - □□□ Systems and equipment malfunctions - FM 264-265; POH-3
    - □□□ Emergency approach and landing - FM 257-263; POH-3
      _____

4. New items
    - □□□ Steep turns - FM 168-172
    - □□□ Rectangular course - FM 173-180
    - □□□ S-turns - FM 181-186
    - □□□ Turns around a point - FM 187-192
    - □□□ Wake turbulence avoidance - PH 169-176
    - □□□ Additional items at CFI's discretion _____
      _____

5. Postflight critique and preview of next lesson

Completion Standards

The lesson will have been successfully completed when the student demonstrates the proper entry procedures and understands how to maintain a specific ground track during the performance of ground reference maneuvers. Additionally, the student will demonstrate increased proficiency in emergency procedures. The student should be able to maintain altitude, ±200 ft.; airspeed, ±15 kt.; and heading, ±20°.

Instructor's comments:_____

_____

Lesson assignment:_____

_____

Notes:_____

_____

_____

_____

_____

FLIGHT LESSON 7: REVIEW

Objective

To review previous lessons to gain proficiency in the flight maneuvers. Additionally, stalls should be entered from straight flight and turns.

Text References

Private Pilot Flight Maneuvers and Practical Test Prep (FM)
Pilot Handbook (PH)
Pilot's Operating Handbook (POH)

Content

1.   Flight Lesson 6 complete? Yes ___   Copy of lesson placed in student's folder? Yes ___
2.   Preflight briefing
3.   Review items

☐☐☐ Normal and crosswind takeoff and landing - FM 118-134
☐☐☐ Maneuvering during slow flight - FM 206-210; PH 50-51
☐☐☐ Power-off stalls (entered from straight flight and turns) - FM 211-215; PH 72-76
☐☐☐ Power-on stalls (entered from straight flight and turns) - FM 216-220; PH 72-76
☐☐☐ Steep turns - FM 168-172
☐☐☐ Emergency approach and landing - FM 257-263; POH-3
☐☐☐ Turns around a point - FM 187-192
☐☐☐ S-turns - FM 181-186
☐☐☐ Rectangular course - FM 173-180
☐☐☐ Recovery from faulty approaches and landings - FM 129-132
☐☐☐ Additional items at CFI's discretion _____

4.   Postflight critique and preview of next lesson

Completion Standards

The lesson will have been successfully completed when the student demonstrates increased proficiency while performing the maneuvers. During the ground reference maneuvers, the student will maintain altitude, ±200 ft.; airspeed, ±15 kt.

Instructor's comments:_____

_____

Lesson assignment:_____

_____

Notes:_____

_____

_____

_____

_____

_____

_____

_____

_____

FLIGHT LESSON 8: GO-AROUND AND FORWARD SLIP TO A LANDING

Objective

To introduce the student to go-around procedures, forward slip to a landing, and recovery from bouncing and ballooning during landing. Additionally, the student will gain proficiency in takeoffs and landings through concentrated practice.

Text References

Private Pilot Flight Maneuvers and Practical Test Prep (FM)
Pilot Handbook (PH)
Pilot's Operating Handbook (POH)

Content

1. Flight Lesson 7 complete? Yes ___   Copy of lesson placed in student's folder? Yes ___
2. Preflight briefing
3. Review items
    - ☐☐☐ Normal and crosswind takeoffs and landings - FM 118-134
    - ☐☐☐ Traffic patterns - FM 103-106; PH 166-168
    - ☐☐☐ Recovery from bouncing and ballooning during landing - FM 129-131
    _____

4. New items
    - ☐☐☐ Go-around - FM 162-166
    - ☐☐☐ Forward slip to a landing - FM 157-161
    - ☐☐☐ Dealing with unexpected requests from ATC - CFI
        - ☐☐☐ Cross airport to opposite downwind - CFI
        - ☐☐☐ Reverse direction on downwind - CFI
        - ☐☐☐ Teardrop maneuver back to final approach from the upwind leg due to a runway change - CFI
    - ☐☐☐ ATC light signals - FM 102
    - ☐☐☐ Wind shear avoidance - FM 103-104
    - ☐☐☐ Additional items at CFI's discretion _____
    _____

5. Postflight critique and preview of next lesson

Completion Standards

The lesson will have been successfully completed when the student can demonstrate an understanding of the go-around procedures, forward slip to a landing, and the recovery from bouncing and ballooning during a landing. Additionally, the student will demonstrate the ability to fly a specific ground track during the performance of ground reference maneuvers. In the traffic pattern, the student will be able to maintain altitude, ±200 ft.; airspeed, ±15 kt.; and desired heading, ±20°.

Instructor's comments:_____

_____

Lesson assignment:_____

_____

Notes:_____

_____

_____

_____

_____

FLIGHT LESSON 9: PRESOLO REVIEW

Objective

To review and to further develop the student's proficiency in the maneuvers and procedures required for solo flight.

Text References

Private Pilot Flight Maneuvers and Practical Test Prep (FM)
Pilot Handbook (PH)
Pilot's Operating Handbook (POH)

Content

1. Flight Lesson 8 complete? Yes ___   Copy of lesson placed in student's folder? Yes ___
2. Preflight briefing
3. Review items

   ☐☐☐ Certificates and documents - FM 41-45
   ☐☐☐ Airplane systems - FM 68-71; PH 79-140; POH-7
   ☐☐☐ Preflight inspection - FM 78-82
   ☐☐☐ Engine starting - FM 86-89
   ☐☐☐ Taxiing - FM 90-94
   ☐☐☐ Before-takeoff check - FM 95-98
   ☐☐☐ Radio communications - FM 99-102; PH 181-184
   ☐☐☐ Traffic patterns - FM 103-106; PH 166-168
   ☐☐☐ Airport and runway markings - PH 142-155
   ☐☐☐ Normal and crosswind takeoff and climb - FM 110-117
   ☐☐☐ Flight by reference to instruments - FM 19-26, 228-243
   ☐☐☐ Maneuvering during slow slight - FM 206-210; PH 50-51

   ☐☐☐ Power-off stalls (entered from straight flight and turns) - FM 211-215; PH 72-76
   ☐☐☐ Power-on stalls (entered from straight flight and turns) - FM 216-220; PH 72-76
   ☐☐☐ Steep turns - FM 168-172
   ☐☐☐ Normal and crosswind approach and landing - FM 118-134
   ☐☐☐ Go-around - FM 162-166
   ☐☐☐ Forward slip to a landing - FM 157-161
   ☐☐☐ Recovery from bouncing or ballooning during landing - FM 129-131
   ☐☐☐ ATC light signals - FM 102
   ☐☐☐ Additional items at CFI's discretion _____
   _____
   _____

4. Postflight critique and preview of next lesson

Completion Standards

The lesson will have been successfully completed when the student displays the ability to perform all of the maneuvers safely, without instructor assistance, in preparation for solo flight in the local practice area. At no time will the successful outcome of each task be in doubt.

Instructor's comments:_____

_____

Lesson assignment:_____

_____

Notes:_____

_____

_____

_____

_____

_____

_____

FLIGHT LESSON 10: PRESOLO REVIEW

Objective

The instructor will evaluate and correct any deficiency in the student's performance of the presolo maneuvers in preparation for solo flight.

Text References

Private Pilot Flight Maneuvers and Practical Test Prep (FM)
Pilot Handbook (PH)
Pilot's Operating Handbook (POH)

Content

1. Flight Lesson 9 complete? Yes ___   Copy of lesson placed in student's folder? Yes ___
2. Preflight briefing
3. Review items

    ☐☐☐ Use of checklists - FM 81; POH-4
    ☐☐☐ Cockpit management - FM 83-85
    ☐☐☐ Normal and crosswind takeoff and climb - FM 110-117
    ☐☐☐ Wake turbulence avoidance - PH 169-176
    ☐☐☐ Collision avoidance - PH 176-181
    ☐☐☐ Wind shear avoidance - FM 103-104
    ☐☐☐ Emergency descent - FM 255-256; POH-3
    ☐☐☐ Emergency approach and landing - FM 257-263; POH-3
    ☐☐☐ Systems and equipment malfunctions - FM 264-265; POH-3
    ☐☐☐ S-turns - FM 181-186
    ☐☐☐ Turns around a point - FM 187-192

    ☐☐☐ Traffic patterns - FM 103-106; PH 166-168
    ☐☐☐ Normal and crosswind approach and landing - FM 118-134
    ☐☐☐ Dealing with unexpected requests from ATC (if appropriate) - CFI
    ☐☐☐ Forward slip to a landing - FM 157-161
    ☐☐☐ Go-around - FM 162-166
    ☐☐☐ After-landing procedures - FM 284
    ☐☐☐ Parking and securing the airplane - FM 285-288
    ☐☐☐ Additional items at CFI's discretion _____
    _____
    _____

4. Postflight critique and preview of next lesson

Completion Standards

The lesson will have been successfully completed when the student displays the ability to perform all of the maneuvers safely, without instructor assistance, in preparation for solo flight in the local practice area. At no time will the successful outcome of each task be in doubt.

Instructor's comments:_____

_____

Lesson assignment:_____

_____

Notes:_____

FLIGHT LESSON 11: FIRST SOLO

Objective

To develop the student's proficiency to a level that will allow the safe accomplishment of the first supervised solo in the traffic pattern.

Text References

Private Pilot Flight Maneuvers and Practical Test Prep (FM)
Pilot Handbook (PH)
Pilot's Operating Handbook (POH)

Content

1. Flight Lesson 10 complete? Yes ___   Copy of lesson and presolo knowledge test placed in student's folder? Yes ___

2. Preflight briefing
    ☐☐☐ Presolo knowledge test - CFI
    ☐☐☐ Instructor endorsements - CFI
    _____

3. Review items (dual)
    ☐☐☐ Radio communication procedures - FM 99-102, PH 181-184
    ☐☐☐ Wake turbulence avoidance - PH 169-176
    ☐☐☐ Normal and crosswind takeoff and climb - FM 110-117
    ☐☐☐ Traffic patterns - FM 103-106; PH 166-168
    ☐☐☐ Normal and crosswind approach and landing - FM 118-134
    ☐☐☐ Go-around - FM 162-166
    _____

4. New items (solo in traffic pattern)
    ☐☐☐ Radio communication procedures - FM 99-102, PH 181-184
    ☐☐☐ Traffic patterns - FM 103-106; PH 166-168
    ☐☐☐ Normal and crosswind takeoff and climb (3) - FM 110-117
    ☐☐☐ Normal and crosswind approach and landing to a full stop (3) - FM 118-134
    ☐☐☐ Postflight procedures - FM 284-288
    ☐☐☐ Additional items at CFI's discretion _____
    _____

5. Postflight critique and preview of next lesson

Completion Standards

The lesson will have been successfully completed when the student completes the presolo knowledge test satisfactorily and safely accomplishes the first supervised solo in the traffic pattern.

Instructor's comments:_____

_____

Lesson assignment:_____

_____

Notes:_____

_____

_____

_____

_____

FLIGHT LESSON 12: STAGE ONE CHECK

Objective

During this stage check, an authorized flight instructor will determine if the student can safely conduct solo flights to the practice area and exercise the privileges associated with the solo operation of the airplane.

Text References

Private Pilot Flight Maneuvers and Practical Test Prep (FM)
Pilot Handbook (PH)
Pilot's Operating Handbook (POH)

Content

1. Flight Lesson 11 complete? Yes ___   Copy of lesson placed in student's folder? Yes ___
2. Preflight briefing
3. Stage check tasks

   ☐☐☐ Airplane systems - FM 68-71; PH 79-140; POH-7
   ☐☐☐ Preflight inspection - FM 78-82
   ☐☐☐ Cockpit management - FM 83-85
   ☐☐☐ Engine starting - FM 86-89
   ☐☐☐ Radio communications - FM 99-102; PH 181-184
   ☐☐☐ Taxiing - FM 90-94
   ☐☐☐ Before-takeoff check - FM 95-98
   ☐☐☐ Wake turbulence avoidance - PH 169-176
   ☐☐☐ Normal and crosswind takeoff and climb - FM 110-117
   ☐☐☐ Collision avoidance - PH 176-181
   ☐☐☐ Wind shear avoidance - FM 103-104
   ☐☐☐ Flight by reference to instruments - FM 19-26, 228-243

   ☐☐☐ Maneuvering during slow flight - FM 206-210; PH 50-51
   ☐☐☐ Power-off stall - FM 211-215; PH 72-76
   ☐☐☐ Power-on stall - FM 216-220; PH 72-76
   ☐☐☐ Systems and equipment malfunctions - FM 264-265; POH-3
   ☐☐☐ Emergency approach and landing - FM 257-263; POH-3
   ☐☐☐ Traffic patterns - FM 103-106; PH 166-168
   ☐☐☐ Normal and crosswind approach and landing - FM 118-134
   ☐☐☐ Go around - FM 162-166
   ☐☐☐ Postflight procedures - FM 284-287
   ☐☐☐ Additional items at CFI's discretion _____
   _____
   _____

4. Postflight critique and preview of next lesson

Completion Standards

The lesson and Stage One will have been successfully completed when the student is competent to conduct safe solo flights at the local airport and in the practice area. The student should maintain altitude, ±150 ft.; airspeed, ±10 kt.; and heading, ±20°.

Instructor's comments:_____

_____

Lesson assignment:_____

_____

Notes:_____

_____

_____

_____

_____

STAGE TWO

Stage Two Objective

The student will be introduced to soft- and short-field takeoffs and landings and night-flying operations. Additionally, the student will be instructed in the conduct of cross-country flights in an airplane using pilotage, dead reckoning, and navigation systems while operating under VFR within the U.S. National Airspace System. Finally, the student will receive instruction in preparation for the private pilot (airplane single-engine land) practical test.

Stage Two Completion Standards

The stage will be completed when the student demonstrates proficiency in soft- and short-field takeoffs and landings. Additionally, the student will demonstrate the ability to conduct night flights safely and plan and safely conduct solo cross-country flights in an airplane using pilotage, dead reckoning, and navigation systems while operating under VFR. Finally, the student will demonstrate proficiency in all tasks of the private pilot airplane (single-engine land) practical test and meet or exceed the minimum acceptable standards for the private pilot certificate.

Lesson	Topic
13	Second Solo
14	Short-Field and Soft-Field Takeoffs and Landings
15	Solo Maneuvers Review
16	Navigation Systems
17	Dual Cross-Country
18	Night Flight -- Local
19	Night Cross-Country
20	Solo Cross-Country
20A	Solo Cross-Country (Part 61)
20B	Solo Cross-Country (Part 61)
21	Maneuvers Review
22	Solo Practice
23	Maneuvers Review
24	Solo Practice
25	Stage Two Check

FLIGHT LESSON 13: SECOND SOLO

Objective

To review previous lessons and to accomplish the student's second supervised solo in the traffic pattern.

Text References

Private Pilot Flight Maneuvers and Practical Test Prep (FM)
Pilot Handbook (PH)
Pilot's Operating Handbook (POH)

Content

1. Flight Lesson 12 complete? Yes ___   Copy of lesson placed in student's folder? Yes ___
2. Preflight briefing
3. Review items (dual)
   ☐☐☐ Normal and crosswind takeoff and climb - FM 110-117
   ☐☐☐ Emergency approach and landing - FM 257-263; POH-3
   ☐☐☐ S-turns - FM 181-186
   ☐☐☐ Turns around a point - FM 187-192
   ☐☐☐ Normal and crosswind approach and landing - FM 118-134
   ☐☐☐ Forward slip to a landing - FM 157-161
   ☐☐☐ Go-around - FM 162-166
   _____

4. Review items (second solo in traffic pattern)
   ☐☐☐ Radio communications - FM 99-102; PH 181-184
   ☐☐☐ Normal and/or crosswind takeoff and climb (3) - FM 110-117
   ☐☐☐ Traffic patterns - FM 103-106; PH 166-168
   ☐☐☐ Normal and/or crosswind approach and landing (3 to full stop) - FM 118-134
   ☐☐☐ Postflight procedures - FM 284-288
   ☐☐☐ Additional items at CFI's discretion _____
   _____

5. Postflight critique and preview of next lesson

Completion Standards

The lesson will have been successfully completed when the student demonstrates solo competence in the maneuvers performed and safely accomplishes the second supervised solo in the traffic pattern. The student will maintain altitude, ±150 ft.; airspeed, ±10 kt.; and heading, ±10°.

Instructor's comments:_____

_____

Lesson assignment:_____

_____

Notes:_____

_____

_____

_____

_____

_____

_____

FLIGHT LESSON 14: SHORT-FIELD AND SOFT-FIELD TAKEOFFS AND LANDINGS

Objective

To introduce the student to the procedures and technique required for short-field and soft-field takeoffs and landings.

Text References

Private Pilot Flight Maneuvers and Practical Test Prep (FM)
Pilot Handbook (PH)
Pilot's Operating Handbook (POH)

Content

1. Flight Lesson 13 complete? Yes ___   Copy of lesson placed in student's folder? Yes ___
2. Preflight briefing
3. Review items
   □□□ Maneuvering during slow flight - FM 206-210; PH 50-51
   □□□ Power-off stalls - FM 211-215; PH 72-76
   □□□ Power-on stalls - FM 216-220; PH 72-76
   □□□ Spin awareness - FM 221-222; PH 77-78; POH-3
   □□□ Emergency approach and landing - FM 257-263; POH-3
   □□□ S-turns - FM 181-186
   □□□ Turns around a point - FM 187-192
   □□□ Steep turns - FM 168-172
   _____

4. New items
   □□□ Short-field takeoff and climb - FM 146-151
   □□□ Short-field approach and landing - FM 152-156
   □□□ Soft-field takeoff and climb - FM 135-140
   □□□ Soft-field approach and landing - FM 141-145
   □□□ Additional items at CFI's discretion _____
   _____

5. Postflight critique and preview of next lesson

Completion Standards

The lesson will have been successfully completed when the student can explain when it would be necessary to use short-field or soft-field takeoff and landing procedures. Additionally, the student should be able to demonstrate an understanding of these procedures. The student will maintain the desired altitude, ±150 ft.; airspeed, ±10 kt.; and heading, ±10°.

Instructor's comments:_____

_____

Lesson assignment:_____

_____

Notes:_____

_____

_____

_____

_____

_____

FLIGHT LESSON 15: SOLO MANEUVERS REVIEW

Objective

To develop the student's confidence and proficiency through solo practice of assigned maneuvers.

Text References

Private Pilot Flight Maneuvers and Practical Test Prep (FM)
Pilot Handbook (PH)

Content

1. Flight Lesson 14 complete? Yes ___   Copy of lesson placed in student's folder? Yes ___
2. Preflight briefing
3. Review items

    ☐☐☐ Normal and crosswind takeoff and climb - FM 110-117
    ☐☐☐ Maneuvering during slow flight - FM 206-210; PH 50-51
    ☐☐☐ Power-off stalls - FM 211-215; PH 72-76
    ☐☐☐ Power-on stalls - FM 216-220; PH 72-76
    ☐☐☐ Steep turns - FM 168-172
    ☐☐☐ S-turns - FM 181-186
    ☐☐☐ Turns around a point - FM 187-192
    ☐☐☐ Normal and crosswind approach and landing - FM 118-134
    ☐☐☐ Additional items at CFI's discretion _____

    _____

4. Postflight critique and preview of next lesson

Completion Standards

The lesson will have been successfully completed when the student completes the listed maneuvers assigned for the solo flight. The student will gain confidence and proficiency as a result of the solo practice.

Instructor's comments:_____

_____

Lesson assignment:_____

_____

Notes:_____

_____

_____

_____

_____

_____

_____

_____

_____

_____

_____

FLIGHT LESSON 16: NAVIGATION SYSTEMS

Objective

To introduce the student to the proper use of the navigation system(s) installed in the airplane to determine position and track a specified course. Additionally, the student is introduced to more maneuvers while controlling the airplane with reference to the instruments.

Text References

Private Pilot Flight Maneuvers and Practical Test Prep (FM)
Pilot Handbook (PH)
Navigation equipment operation manual(s)

Content

1. Flight Lesson 15 complete? Yes ___   Copy of lesson placed in student's folder? Yes ___
2. Preflight briefing
3. Review items

   ☐☐☐ Soft-field takeoff and climb - FM 135-140
   ☐☐☐ Maneuvering during slow flight -
       FM 206-210

   ☐☐☐ Power-off stalls - FM 211-215; PH 72-76
   ☐☐☐ Power-on stalls - FM 216-220; PH 72-76
   ☐☐☐ Soft-field approach and landing - FM 141-145

4. New items

   ☐☐☐ VOR orientation and tracking - FM 197-198;
       PH 484-495
   ☐☐☐ ADF orientation and tracking - FM 197-198;
       PH 497-503
   ☐☐☐ LORAN orientation and tracking -
       FM 197-198; PH 505-508
   ☐☐☐ GPS orientation and tracking - FM 197-198;
       PH 508-514
   ☐☐☐ Maneuvering during slow flight (IR) -
       FM 206-210

   ☐☐☐ Power-off stalls (IR) - FM 211-215
   ☐☐☐ Power-on stalls (IR) - FM 216-220
   ☐☐☐ Recovery from unusual flight attitudes (IR) -
       FM 244-249
   ☐☐☐ Radio communications, navigation systems/
       facilities, and radar services (IR) -
       FM 250-252
   ☐☐☐ Additional items at CFI's discretion _____
       _____
       _____

5. Postflight critique and preview of next lesson

Completion Standards

This lesson will have been successfully completed when the student displays an understanding of the navigation system(s) in the airplane. Additionally, the student will use the correct recovery procedure from unusual attitudes and will be able to maintain control of the airplane by instrument reference and by the use of navigation systems, radio communications, and radar services. All approaches will be stabilized, and the student will maintain the desired airspeed, +10/–5 kt.

Instructor's comments:_____

_____

Lesson assignment:_____

_____

Notes:_____

_____

_____

_____

_____

_____

FLIGHT LESSON 17: DUAL CROSS-COUNTRY

Objective

To introduce the student to cross-country procedures that include flight planning, pilotage and dead reckoning, navigation systems, diversion to an alternate airport, and lost procedures.

Text References

Private Pilot Flight Maneuvers and Practical Test Prep (FM) Sectional chart
Pilot Handbook (PH) *Airport/Facility Directory*
Pilot's Operating Handbook (POH)

Content

1. Flight Lesson 16 complete? Yes ___   Copy of lesson placed in student's folder? Yes ___
2. Preflight briefing
3. Review items

   ☐☐☐ Navigation system(s) - FM 197-198; PH 479-514
   ☐☐☐ Emergency descent - FM 255-256; POH-3
   ☐☐☐ Emergency approach and landing - FM 257-263; POH-3
   ☐☐☐ Systems & equipment malfunctions - FM 264-265; POH-3

   ☐☐☐ Emergency equipment and survival gear - FM 266-267
   ☐☐☐ Short-field takeoffs and landings - FM 146-156
   ☐☐☐ Soft-field takeoffs and landings - FM 135-145
   ☐☐☐ Forward slip to a landing - FM 157-161
   ☐☐☐ Wind shear avoidance - FM 103-104
   ☐☐☐ Wake turbulence avoidance - PH 169-176

4. New items

   ☐☐☐ Aeronautical charts - PH 427-440
   ☐☐☐ *Airport/Facility Directory*, Notice to Airmen (NOTAM), and other publications - PH 441-449
   ☐☐☐ National Airspace System - PH 201-212
   ☐☐☐ Route selection - FM 51-54; PH 515-521
   ☐☐☐ Navigation log - PH 531
   ☐☐☐ Obtaining weather information - FM 46-50; PH 383-426
   ☐☐☐ Determining performance and limitations - FM 61-63; PH 295-324; POH-2, 5
   ☐☐☐ Cockpit management - FM 83-85
   ☐☐☐ Weight and balance computations - PH 313-324; POH-6
   ☐☐☐ Aeromedical factors - PH 325-358
   ☐☐☐ Filing a VFR flight plan - PH 522-524; CFI
   ☐☐☐ Course interception - FM 194-195
   ☐☐☐ Open VFR flight plan - CFI
   ☐☐☐ Pilotage and dead reckoning - FM 193-196; PH 515-521, 524-530

   ☐☐☐ VFR radar services, as appropriate - FM 197-198; PH 196-201
   ☐☐☐ Setting power and fuel mixture - POH-4, 5
   ☐☐☐ Estimating in-flight visibility - CFI
   ☐☐☐ Operational problems associated with varying terrain features during the flight - CFI
   ☐☐☐ Recognition of critical weather situations - CFI
   ☐☐☐ Computing groundspeed, ETA, and fuel consumption - PH 453-460
   ☐☐☐ Obtaining in-flight weather information - PH 400-403
   ☐☐☐ Unfamiliar airport operations - CFI
   ☐☐☐ Lost procedures - FM 202-204; PH 527-530
   ☐☐☐ Diversion to alternate airport - FM 199-201; PH 525-527
   ☐☐☐ Closing a VFR flight plan - PH 524; CFI
   ☐☐☐ Additional items at CFI's discretion _____
   _____
   _____

5. Postflight critique and preview of next lesson

Completion Standards

This lesson will have been successfully completed when the student, with instructor assistance, is able to perform the cross-country flight planning and fly the planned course making necessary off-course corrections and computing groundspeed, ETA, and fuel consumption. The student will display the ability to navigate by means of pilotage and dead reckoning and by any other navigation system. Additionally, the student will understand how to perform lost procedures and a diversion to an alternate airport.

Instructor's comments:_____

_____

Lesson assignment:_____

_____

Notes:_____

FLIGHT LESSON 18: NIGHT FLIGHT -- LOCAL

Objective

To introduce the student to night-flying preparation and night-flying operations.

Text References

Private Pilot Flight Maneuvers and Practical Test Prep (FM)
Pilot Handbook (PH)
Pilot's Operating Handbook (POH)

Content

1.   Flight Lesson 17 complete? Yes ___   Copy of lesson placed in student's folder? Yes ___
2.   Preflight briefing
3.   New items

☐☐☐ Aeromedical factors associated with night flying - PH 336-341
☐☐☐ Airport lighting - PH 156-164
☐☐☐ Airplane equipment and lighting requirements - FM 272-273
☐☐☐ Personal equipment and preparation - FM 273
☐☐☐ Safety precautions while on the ground and in the air - FM 275
☐☐☐ Emergency procedures at night - FM 275
☐☐☐ Night preflight inspection - FM 276-277
☐☐☐ Cockpit management - FM 83-85
☐☐☐ Engine starting - FM 278
☐☐☐ Taxiing - FM 278
☐☐☐ Before-takeoff check - FM 278
☐☐☐ Normal takeoffs and landings - FM 110-134, 279-282
☐☐☐ Soft-field takeoffs and landings - FM 135-145, 279-282

☐☐☐ Short-field takeoffs and landings - FM 146-156, 279-282
☐☐☐ Traffic patterns - FM 281-282; PH 166-168
☐☐☐ Go-around - FM 162-166
☐☐☐ Collision avoidance - PH 176-181
☐☐☐ Steep turns - FM 168-172; PH 53-54
☐☐☐ Maneuvering during slow flight - FM 206-210; PH 50-51
☐☐☐ Power-off stalls - FM 211-215; PH 72-76
☐☐☐ Power-on stalls - FM 216-220; PH 72-76
☐☐☐ Recovery from unusual flight attitudes (IR) - FM 244-249
☐☐☐ Systems and equipment malfunctions - FM 264-265; POH-3
☐☐☐ Emergency approach and landing - FM 257-263; POH-3
☐☐☐ Additional items at CFI's discretion _____

_____
_____

4.   Postflight critique and preview of next lesson

Completion Standards

The lesson will have been successfully completed when the student displays the ability to maintain orientation in the local practice area and airport traffic pattern, and can accurately interpret aircraft and airport lights. The student will maintain altitude, ±150 ft.; airspeed, ±10 kt.; and heading, ±10°.

Instructor's comments:_____

_____

Lesson assignment:_____

_____

Notes:_____

_____

_____

_____

_____

FLIGHT LESSON 19: NIGHT CROSS-COUNTRY

Objective

To develop the student's ability to plan and fly a night cross-country flight of more than 100 NM total distance with at least one landing at an unfamiliar airport; to develop the student's proficiency in navigating at night by means of pilotage, dead reckoning, and other navigation system(s).

Text References

Private Pilot Flight Maneuvers and Practical Test Prep (FM)   Sectional chart
Pilot Handbook (PH)   *Airport/Facility Directory*
Pilot's Operating Handbook (POH)

Content

1. Flight Lesson 18 complete? Yes ___   Copy of lesson placed in student's folder? Yes ___
2. Preflight briefing
3. Review items

☐☐☐ Aeromedical factors - FM 72-76; PH 325-341

☐☐☐ Personal equipment and preparation - FM 273

☐☐☐ Obtaining weather information - FM 46-50; PH 383-426

☐☐☐ Determining performance and limitation - FM 61-63; PH 295-324; POH-2, 4, 5, 6

☐☐☐ Short-field takeoffs and landings - FM 146-156

☐☐☐ Soft-field takeoffs and landings - FM 135-145

☐☐☐ Go-around - FM 162-166

☐☐☐ Straight-and-level (IR) - FM 228-231

☐☐☐ Turns to headings (IR) - FM 241-243

☐☐☐ Constant airspeed descent/climb (IR) - FM 232-240

☐☐☐ Navigation systems, ATC services (IR) - FM 250-252

☐☐☐ Collision avoidance procedures - PH 176-181

☐☐☐ Pilotage and dead reckoning - FM 193-196; PH 515-521, 524-530

☐☐☐ Navigation systems - FM 197-198; PH 479-514

☐☐☐ Unfamiliar airport operations - CFI

☐☐☐ Lost procedures - FM 202-204; PH 527-530

☐☐☐ Diversion to an alternate airport - FM 199-201; PH 525-527

4. New items

☐☐☐ Route selection - FM 274

☐☐☐ Night VFR fuel requirements (FAR 91.151) - PH 269

☐☐☐ Additional items at CFI's discretion _____

5. Postflight critique and preview of next lesson

☐ Instructor endorse student pilot certificate and logbook for solo cross-country

Completion Standards

The lesson will have been successfully completed when the student demonstrates the proficiency to conduct safe solo cross-country flights. The student will maintain altitude, ±200 ft.; airspeed, ±10 kt.; established heading, ±15°; and remain within 3 NM of the planned route at all times. Additionally, at the completion of this lesson, the student will have a total of at least 3 hr. of night flight training and 10 takeoffs and 10 landings to a full stop. The instructor will endorse the student's pilot certificate and logbook for cross-country privileges.

Instructor's comments:_____

_____

Lesson assignment:_____

_____

Notes:_____

_____

_____

FLIGHT LESSON 20: SOLO CROSS-COUNTRY

Objective

To increase the student's confidence and proficiency in the conduct of cross-country flights. This solo cross-country flight should be at least 100 NM (150 NM for Part 61 students) total distance with full-stop landings at a minimum of three points, and one segment of the flight should consist of a straight-line distance of at least 50 NM between the takeoff and landing locations.

Text References

Private Pilot Flight Maneuvers and Practical Test Prep (FM)
Pilot Handbook (PH)
Pilot's Operating Handbook (POH)

Content

1.   Flight Lesson 19 complete? Yes ___   Copy of lesson placed in student's folder? Yes ___
2.   Preflight briefing
    ☐ Instructor review of student's cross-country planning - CFI
    ☐ Instructor logbook endorsement - CFI
3.   Review items

☐☐☐ Obtaining weather information - FM 46-50; PH 383-426

☐☐☐ Cross-country flight planning - FM 51-54; PH 515-532

☐☐☐ Determining performance and limitations - FM 61-63; PH 295-324; POH - 2, 4, 5, 6

☐☐☐ Pilotage and dead reckoning - FM 193-196; PH 515-521, 524-530

☐☐☐ Navigation systems - FM 197-198; PH 479-514

☐☐☐ Computing groundspeed, ETA, and fuel consumption - PH 453-460

☐☐☐ Short-field takeoffs and landings - FM 146-156

☐☐☐ Soft-field takeoffs and landings - FM 135-145

☐☐☐ Landing at a minimum of three airports - CFI

☐☐☐ Additional items at CFI's discretion _____

_____

_____

4.   Postflight critique and preview of next lesson

Completion Standards

The lesson will have been successfully completed when the student can properly plan and conduct the solo cross-country flight using pilotage, dead reckoning, and navigation systems. During the postflight critique, the instructor should determine how well the flight was conducted through oral questioning. The student will have made at least three (3) takeoffs and landings to a full stop at an airport with an operating control tower by the end of this lesson.

Instructor's comments:_____

_____

Lesson assignment:_____

_____

Notes:_____

_____

_____

_____

_____

_____

FLIGHT LESSON 20A: SOLO CROSS-COUNTRY (PART 61)

Objective

To increase the student's proficiency in the conduct of solo cross-country flights. A landing must be conducted at an airport that is at a straight-line distance of more than 50 NM from the original departure airport.

Text References

Private Pilot Flight Maneuvers and Practical Test Prep (FM)
Pilot Handbook (PH)
Pilot's Operating Handbook (POH)

Content

1. Flight Lesson 20 complete? Yes ___   Copy of lesson placed in student's folder? Yes ___
2. Preflight briefing
   - ☐ Instructor review of student's cross-country planning - CFI
   - ☐ Instructor logbook endorsement - CFI

3. Review items
   - ☐☐☐ Obtaining weather information - FM 46-50; PH 383-426
   - ☐☐☐ Cross-country flight planning - FM 51-54; PH 515-532
   - ☐☐☐ Determining performance and limitations - FM 61-63; PH 295-324; POH-2, 4, 5, 6
   - ☐☐☐ Short-field takeoffs and landings - FM 146-156
   - ☐☐☐ Soft-field takeoffs and landings - FM 135-145
   - ☐☐☐ Pilotage and dead reckoning - FM 193-196; PH 515-521, 524-530
   - ☐☐☐ Navigation systems and radar services - FM 197-198; PH 196-201, 479-514
   - ☐☐☐ Computing groundspeed, ETAs, and fuel consumption - PH 453-460
   - ☐☐☐ Tower and/or nontower airport operations - PH 164-168, 184-193
   - ☐☐☐ Landing at an airport more than 50 NM from airport of departure - CFI
   - ☐☐☐ Additional items at CFI's discretion _____

   _____

   _____

4. Postflight critique and preview of next lesson

Completion Standards

The lesson will have been successfully completed when the student completes this cross-country flight as planned. During the postflight critique, the instructor will determine how well the flight was conducted through oral questioning.

Instructor's comments:_____

_____

Lesson assignment:_____

_____

Notes:_____

_____

_____

_____

_____

_____

_____

FLIGHT LESSON 20B: SOLO CROSS-COUNTRY (PART 61)

Objective

To increase the student's confidence in the conduct of solo cross-country flights.

Text References

Private Pilot Flight Maneuvers and Practical Test Prep (FM)
Pilot Handbook (PH)
Pilot's Operating Handbook (POH)

> In the event 40 hours of total time is an objective, 1 hour of solo practice may be substituted for this 2-hour cross-country flight.

Content

1. Flight Lesson 20A complete? Yes ___   Copy of lesson placed in student's folder? Yes ___
2. Preflight briefing
   - ☐ Instructor review of student's cross-country planning - CFI
   - ☐ Instructor logbook endorsement - CFI

3. Review items
   - ☐☐☐ Obtaining weather information - FM 46-50; PH 383-426
   - ☐☐☐ Cross-country flight planning - FM 51-54; PH 515-532
   - ☐☐☐ Determining performance and limitations - FM 61-63; PH 295-324; POH-2, 4, 5, 6
   - ☐☐☐ Pilotage and dead reckoning - FM 193-196; PH 515-521, 524-530
   - ☐☐☐ Navigation systems and radar services - FM 197-198; PH 196-201, 479-514

   - ☐☐☐ Computing groundspeed, ETAs, and fuel consumption - PH 453-460
   - ☐☐☐ Short-field takeoffs and landings - FM 146-156
   - ☐☐☐ Soft-field takeoffs and landings - FM 135-145
   - ☐☐☐ Landing at an airport more than 50 NM from airport of departure - CFI
   - ☐☐☐ Additional items at CFI's discretion _____
   _____
   _____

4. Postflight critique and preview of next lesson

Completion Standards

The lesson will have been successfully completed when the student completes this cross-country flight as planned. During the postflight critique, the instructor will determine how well the flight was conducted through oral questioning. At completion of this lesson, the student will have at least 5 hr. of solo cross-country flight time.

Instructor's comments:_____

_____

Lesson assignment:_____

_____

Notes:_____

_____

_____

_____

_____

_____

_____

FLIGHT LESSON 21: MANEUVERS REVIEW

Objective

To determine the student's proficiency level in the maneuvers and procedures covered previously.

Text References

Private Pilot Flight Maneuvers and Practical Test Prep (FM)
Pilot Handbook (PH)
Pilot's Operating Handbook (POH)

Content

1. Flight Lesson 20/20A/20B (as appropriate) complete? Yes ___
   Copy of lesson(s) placed in student's folder? Yes ___
2. Preflight briefing
3. Review items

   ☐☐☐ Airplane logbook entries - FM 43
       ☐☐☐ Airworthiness requirements - FM 45-49
   ☐☐☐ Operation of systems - FM 64-67; PH 30-41; 79-140
   ☐☐☐ Preflight inspection - FM 78-82
   ☐☐☐ Cockpit management - FM 83-85
   ☐☐☐ Engine starting - FM 86-89
   ☐☐☐ Radio communications - FM 99-102; PH 181-184
   ☐☐☐ Airport and runway markings and lighting - PH 142-164
   ☐☐☐ Taxiing - FM 90-94
   ☐☐☐ Before-takeoff check - FM 95-98
   ☐☐☐ Short-field takeoff and climb - FM 146-151
   ☐☐☐ Soft-field takeoff and climb - FM 135-140
   ☐☐☐ Steep turns - FM 168-172
   ☐☐☐ Maneuvering during slow flight - FM 206-210; PH 50-51

   ☐☐☐ Power-off stalls - FM 211-215; PH 72-76
   ☐☐☐ Power-on stalls - FM 216-220; PH 72-76
   ☐☐☐ Spin awareness - FM 221-222; PH 77-78; POH-3
   ☐☐☐ Emergency descent - FM 255-256; POH-3
   ☐☐☐ Emergency approach and landing - FM 257-263; POH-3
   ☐☐☐ Systems and equipment malfunctions - FM 264-265; POH-3
   ☐☐☐ Traffic patterns - FM 103-106; PH 166-168
   ☐☐☐ Short-field approach and landing - FM 152-156
   ☐☐☐ Soft-field approach and landing - FM 141-145
   ☐☐☐ Go-around - FM 162-166
   ☐☐☐ Forward slip to a landing - FM 157-161
   ☐☐☐ After-landing procedures - FM 284
   ☐☐☐ Parking and securing the airplane - FM 285-288
   ☐☐☐ Additional items at CFI's discretion _____
   _____
   _____

4. Postflight critique and preview of next lesson

Completion Standards

The lesson will have been successfully completed when the student demonstrates improved proficiency in the various tasks given. The student will maintain the altitude, airspeed, and heading standards specified for the appropriate task in the current FAA Private Pilot Practical Test Standards.

Instructor's comments:_____

_____

Lesson assignment:_____

_____

Notes:_____

_____

_____

FLIGHT LESSON 22: SOLO PRACTICE

Objective

To further develop the student's proficiency through solo practice of assigned maneuvers.

Text References

Private Pilot Flight Maneuvers and Practical Test Prep (FM)
Pilot Handbook (PH)
Pilot's Operating Handbook (POH)

Content

1. Flight Lesson 21 complete? Yes ___   Copy of lesson placed in student's folder? Yes ___
2. Preflight briefing
3. Review items
   - ☐☐☐ Short-field takeoffs and landings - FM 146-156
   - ☐☐☐ Soft-field takeoffs and landings - FM 135-145
   - ☐☐☐ Steep turns - FM 168-172
   - ☐☐☐ Maneuvering during slow flight - FM 206-210; PH 50-51
   - ☐☐☐ Power-on stalls - FM 216-220; PH 72-76
   - ☐☐☐ Power-off stalls - FM 211-215; PH 72-76
   - ☐☐☐ Traffic patterns - FM 103-106; PH 166-168
   - ☐☐☐ Forward slip to a landing - FM 157-161
   - ☐☐☐ Radio communications - FM 99-102; PH 181-184
   - ☐☐☐ Additional items at CFI's discretion _____

4. Postflight critique and preview of next lesson

Completion Standards

The lesson will have been successfully completed when the student completes the solo flight. The student will gain confidence and improve performance as a result of the solo practice period.

Instructor's comments:_____

_____

Lesson assignment:_____

_____

Notes:_____

_____

_____

_____

_____

_____

_____

_____

_____

_____

_____

FLIGHT LESSON 23: MANEUVERS REVIEW

Objective

To develop improved performance and proficiency in the procedures and maneuvers covered previously.

Text References

Private Pilot Flight Maneuvers and Practical Test Prep (FM)
Pilot Handbook (PH)
Pilot's Operating Handbook (POH)

Content

1. Flight Lesson 22 complete? Yes ___   Copy of lesson placed in student's folder? Yes ___
2. Preflight briefing
3. Review items

☐☐☐ Short-field takeoff and climb - FM 146-151
☐☐☐ Soft-field takeoff and climb - FM 135-140
☐☐☐ Cross-country procedures -
      FM 51-54, 193-204
☐☐☐ Maneuvering during slow flight -
      FM 206-210; PH 50-51
☐☐☐ Power-off stalls - FM 211-215; PH 72-76
☐☐☐ Power-on stalls - FM 216-220; PH 72-76
☐☐☐ Spin awareness - FM 221-222; PH 77-78;
      POH-3
☐☐☐ Straight-and-level flight (IR) - FM 228-231
☐☐☐ Turns to headings (IR) - FM 241-243
☐☐☐ Constant airspeed descents (IR) -
      FM 236-240
☐☐☐ Constant airspeed climbs (IR) - FM 232-235
☐☐☐ Recovery from unusual flight attitudes (IR) -
      FM 244-249

☐☐☐ Radio communications, navigation systems/
      facilities, and radar services (IR) - FM 250-252
☐☐☐ Emergency approach and landing - FM 257-263
☐☐☐ S-turns - FM 181-186
☐☐☐ Turns around a point - FM 187-192
☐☐☐ Traffic patterns - FM 103-106; PH 166-168
☐☐☐ Short-field approach and landing - FM 152-156
☐☐☐ Soft-field approach and landing - FM 141-145
☐☐☐ Go-around - FM 162-166
☐☐☐ Forward slip to a landing - FM 157-161
☐☐☐ Postflight procedures - FM 284-287
☐☐☐ Additional items at CFI's discretion _____
_____

_____

4. Postflight critique and preview of next lesson

Completion Standards

The lesson will have been successfully completed when the student demonstrates improved proficiency in the maneuvers given. The student will complete each task to the standards specified in the current FAA Private Pilot Practical Test Standards.

Instructor's comments:_____

_____

Lesson assignment:_____

_____

Notes:_____

_____

_____

_____

_____

_____

_____

FLIGHT LESSON 24: SOLO PRACTICE

Objective

To further develop the student's proficiency of assigned maneuvers through solo practice.

Text References

Private Pilot Flight Maneuvers and Practical Test Prep (FM)
Pilot Handbook (PH)
Pilot's Operating Handbook (POH)

Content

1. Flight Lesson 23 complete? Yes ___   Copy of lesson placed in student's folder? Yes ___
2. Preflight briefing
3. Review items
    - ☐☐☐ Short-field takeoffs and landings - FM 146-156
    - ☐☐☐ Soft-field takeoffs and landings - FM 135-145
    - ☐☐☐ Maneuvering during slow flight - FM 206-210; PH 50-51
    - ☐☐☐ Power-off stalls - FM 211-215; PH 72-76
    - ☐☐☐ Power-on stalls - FM 216-220; PH 72-76
    - ☐☐☐ Steep turns - FM 168-172
    - ☐☐☐ S-turns - FM 181-186
    - ☐☐☐ Turns around a point - FM 187-192
    - ☐☐☐ Traffic patterns - FM 103-106; PH 166-168
    - ☐☐☐ Forward slip to a landing - FM 157-161
    - ☐☐☐ Maneuvers as assigned by the instructor - CFI
    - ☐☐☐ Additional items at CFI's discretion _____

4. Postflight critique and preview of next lesson

Completion Standards

The lesson will have been successfully completed when the student completes the solo flight. The student will gain confidence and improve performance as a result of the solo practice period.

Instructor's comments:_____

_____

Lesson assignment:_____

_____

Notes:_____

_____

_____

_____

_____

_____

_____

_____

_____

_____

_____

FLIGHT LESSON 25: STAGE TWO CHECK

Objective

The student will be able to demonstrate the required proficiency of a private pilot by utilizing the current FAA Private Pilot Practical Test Standards.

Text References

Private Pilot Flight Maneuvers and Practical Test Prep (FM)
Pilot Handbook (PH)

Content

1. Flight Lesson 24 complete? Yes ___   Copy of lesson placed in student's folder? Yes ___
2. Stage Check Tasks

☐☐☐ Certificates and documents - FM 41-45
　☐☐☐ Airworthiness requirements -
　　FM 45-49
☐☐☐ Obtaining weather info. - FM 46-50;
　PH 383-426
☐☐☐ Cross-country flight planning - FM 51-54
☐☐☐ National Airspace System - FM 55-60
☐☐☐ Determining performance & limitations -
　FM 61-63
☐☐☐ Operation of airplane systems - FM 68-71
☐☐☐ Aeromedical factors - FM 72-76
☐☐☐ Preflight inspection - FM 78-82
☐☐☐ Cockpit management - FM 83-85
☐☐☐ Engine starting - FM 86-89
☐☐☐ Taxiing - FM 90-94
☐☐☐ Before-takeoff check - FM 95-98
☐☐☐ Radio comm. and ATC light signals -
　FM 99-102
☐☐☐ Traffic patterns - FM 103-106
☐☐☐ Airport and runway markings and lighting -
　PH 142-164
☐☐☐ Normal and crosswind takeoff & climb -
　FM 110-117
☐☐☐ Soft-field takeoff and climb - FM 135-140
☐☐☐ Short-field takeoff and climb - FM 146-151
☐☐☐ Pilotage and dead reckoning - FM 193-196
☐☐☐ Nav. systems and radar services - FM 197-198
☐☐☐ Lost procedures - FM 202-204
☐☐☐ Diversion - FM 199-201
☐☐☐ Straight-and-level flight (IR) - FM 228-231
☐☐☐ Constant airspeed climbs (IR) - FM 232-235
☐☐☐ Constant airspeed descents (IR) - FM 236-240

☐☐☐ Turns to headings (IR) - FM 241-243
☐☐☐ Unusual flight attitudes (IR) - FM 244-249
☐☐☐ Radio communications, navigation systems/
　facilities, and radar services (IR) - FM 250-252
☐☐☐ Steep turns - FM 168-172
☐☐☐ Systems and equipment malfunctions -
　FM 264-265
☐☐☐ Maneuvering during slow flight - FM 206-210
☐☐☐ Power-off stalls - FM 211-215
☐☐☐ Power-on stalls - FM 216-220
☐☐☐ Spin awareness - FM 221-222; PH 77-78
☐☐☐ Emergency descent - FM 255-256
☐☐☐ Emergency approach and landing -
　FM 257-263
☐☐☐ Rectangular course - FM 173-180
☐☐☐ S-turns - FM 181-186
☐☐☐ Turns around a point - FM 187-192
☐☐☐ Normal & crosswind approach & landing -
　FM 118-134
☐☐☐ Soft-field approach and landing - FM 141-145
☐☐☐ Short-field approach and landing - FM 152-156
☐☐☐ Forward slip to a landing - FM 157-161
☐☐☐ Go-around - FM 162-166
☐☐☐ After-landing procedures - FM 284
☐☐☐ Parking and securing the airplane - FM 285-288
☐☐☐ Emergency equip. & survival gear - FM 266-267
☐☐☐ Night preparation (oral or flight) - FM 270-275
☐☐☐ Night flight (oral or flight) - FM 276-282
☐☐☐ Additional items at CFI's discretion _____

_____

_____

3. Postflight critique
4. Flight Lesson 25 complete? Yes ___
　Copy of lesson and graduation certificate placed in student's folder? Yes___

Completion Standards

The lesson will have been successfully completed when the student demonstrates the required level of proficiency in all tasks of the current FAA Private Pilot Practical Test Standards. If additional instruction is necessary, the chief flight instructor will assign the additional training. If the flight is satisfactory, the chief flight instructor will complete the student's training records and issue a graduation certificate.

Instructor's comments:_____

_____

Notes:_____

PRESOLO KNOWLEDGE TEST

Airplane make/model: _____

1. List the airspeeds and their definitions for your airplane.

    Airspeed   Definition

    V_{S0} _____   _____

    V_{S1} _____   _____

    V_R _____   _____

    V_X _____   _____

    V_Y _____   _____

    V_{FE} _____   _____

    V_A _____   _____

    V_{NO} _____   _____

    V_{NE} _____   _____

2. The maximum ramp (gross) weight for your airplane is _____ lb.

3. The maximum takeoff weight for your airplane is _____ lb.

4. Fuel: Maximum capacity _____ gal. of which _____ gal. is usable

    Minimum to start a solo flight _____ gal.

    Grade _____

    Color _____

    Optional grades and colors _____

5. Oil: Maximum capacity _____ qt.

    Minimum to start a solo flight _____ qt.

    Grade _____

6. Compute the location of the center of gravity (CG) for a solo flight with full fuel in your airplane. Is the CG within limits?

7. What is the takeoff ground roll and the distance over a 50-ft. obstacle for your airplane at your airport with full fuel, a temperature of 29° C, 5-kt. headwind, and an altimeter setting of 29.64?

8. What is the ground roll and total landing distance over a 50-ft. obstacle for your airplane at your airport with 3/4 fuel, a temperature of 32° C, calm wind, and an altimeter setting of 30.10?

9. What are the indications of carburetor icing? When is carburetor heat recommended to be used in your airplane?

10. What are the radio frequencies used at your airport?

   Clearance Delivery _____

   ATIS _____

   Ground _____

   Tower _____

   Approach/Departure _____

   CTAF _____

   UNICOM _____

   FSS _____

11. At your airport:

   a.   What runways are available?

   b.   What is the direction of the traffic pattern for each runway?

   c.   What is the traffic pattern altitude?

   d.   In what class of airspace is the airport located?

12. How do you enter and depart the traffic pattern at your airport?

13. What radio communication procedures are required at your airport?

14. Explain the procedures you would use to land at your airport if the communication radio(s) failed.

15. List the meaning of the following ATC light signals:

	In Flight	On Surface
Steady green	_____	_____
Flashing green	_____	_____
Steady red	_____	_____
Flashing red	_____	_____
Flashing white	_____	_____
Alternating red and green	_____	_____

16. What airplane certificates and documents must be on board your airplane prior to every flight?

17. What personal documents and endorsements must you have before beginning a solo flight?

18. Who is directly responsible and is the final authority as to the operation of your airplane when you are flying solo?

19. You may not fly as a pilot within _____ hours after the consumption of an alcoholic beverage or with _____% by weight or more alcohol in the blood.

20. Explain the regulatory preflight action requirements.

21. Explain your use of safety belts and shoulder harnesses while flying solo.

22. When aircraft are approaching each other head-on, or nearly so, what action should be taken?

23. Except for takeoff or landing, at what minimum safe altitudes should you operate your airplane?

24. Explain the altimeter setting procedures.

25. When practicing steep turns, slow flight, power-on stalls, and power-off stalls, you should select an altitude that allows the maneuver to be completed no lower than _____.

26. Explain the go-around procedures in your airplane. When would you use the go-around procedures?

27. The best glide airspeed for your airplane (at maximum gross weight) is _____.

    a. What airplane configuration is specified to obtain the maximum glide?

28. Explain the actions you would take if the airplane engine failed in the following situations:

    a. Right after liftoff

    b. During the takeoff climb at an altitude of 100 ft. AGL

    c. En route

29. Explain the recommended use of flaps for takeoff in your airplane.

30. For a student pilot, what are the minimum visibility requirements?

31. For a student pilot, what are the restrictions to flight above clouds?

32. For a student pilot, what are the limitations of carrying passengers?

33. What are the day-VFR fuel requirements?

END OF EXAM

STAGE ONE KNOWLEDGE TEST

The figures on pages 71 through 80 are from the FAA's *Computerized Testing Supplement for Recreational Pilot and Private Pilot* book, which is available from your flight school or instructor.

1. What is the relationship of lift, drag, thrust, and weight when the airplane is in straight-and-level flight?

A — Lift equals weight and thrust equals drag.
B — Lift, drag, and weight equal thrust.
C — Lift and weight equal thrust and drag.

2. In what flight condition must an aircraft be placed in order to spin?

A — Partially stalled with one wing low.
B — In a steep diving spiral.
C — Stalled.

3. What must a pilot be aware of as a result of ground effect?

A — Wingtip vortices increase creating wake turbulence problems for arriving and departing aircraft.
B — Induced drag decreases; therefore, any excess speed at the point of flare may cause considerable floating.
C — A full stall landing will require less up elevator deflection than would a full stall when done free of ground effect.

4. An airplane has been loaded in such a manner that the CG is located aft of the aft CG limit. One undesirable flight characteristic a pilot might experience with this airplane would be

A — a longer takeoff run.
B — difficulty in recovering from a stalled condition.
C — stalling at higher-than-normal airspeed.

5. During an approach to a stall, an increased load factor will cause the airplane to

A — stall at a higher airspeed.
B — have a tendency to spin.
C — be more difficult to control.

6. Which instrument(s) will become inoperative if the static vents become clogged?

A — Airspeed only.
B — Altimeter only.
C — Airspeed, altimeter, and vertical speed.

7. If a flight is made from an area of high pressure into an area of lower pressure without the altimeter setting being adjusted, the altimeter will indicate

A — lower than the actual altitude above sea level.
B — higher than the actual altitude above sea level.
C — the actual altitude above sea level.

8. If an aircraft is equipped with a fixed-pitch propeller and a float-type carburetor, the first indication of carburetor ice would most likely be

A — a drop in oil temperature and cylinder head temperature.
B — engine roughness.
C — loss of RPM.

9. What change occurs in the fuel/air mixture when carburetor heat is applied?

A — A decrease in RPM results from the lean mixture.
B — The fuel/air mixture becomes richer.
C — The fuel/air mixture becomes leaner.

10. If a pilot suspects that the engine (with a fixed-pitch propeller) is detonating during climb-out after takeoff, the initial corrective action to take would be to

A — lean the mixture.
B — lower the nose slightly to increase airspeed.
C — apply carburetor heat.

11. (Refer to figure 12 on page 74.) What is the difference between area A and area E on the airport depicted?

A — "A" may be used for taxi and takeoff; "E" may be used only as an overrun.
B — "A" may be used for all operations except heavy aircraft landings; "E" may be used only as an overrun.
C — "A" may be used only for taxiing; "E" may be used for all operations except landings.

12. (Refer to figure 3 on page 71.) Select the proper traffic pattern and runway for landing. The wind direction indicator is a tetrahedron.

A — Left-hand traffic and Runway 18.
B — Right-hand traffic and Runway 18.
C — Left-hand traffic and Runway 22.

13. The most effective method of scanning for other aircraft for collision avoidance during daylight hours is to use

A — regularly spaced concentration on the 3-, 9-, and 12-o'clock positions.
B — a series of short, regularly spaced eye movements to search each 10-degree sector.
C — peripheral vision by scanning small sectors and utilizing offcenter viewing.

14. If instructed by ground control to taxi to Runway 9, the pilot may proceed

A — via taxiways and across runways to, but not onto, Runway 9.
B — to the next intersecting runway where further clearance is required.
C — via taxiways and across runways to Runway 9, where an immediate takeoff may be made.

15. A steady green light signal directed from the control tower to an aircraft in flight is a signal that the pilot

A — is cleared to land.
B — should give way to other aircraft and continue circling.
C — should return for landing.

16. After takeoff, which airspeed would the pilot use to gain the most altitude in a given period of time?

A — V_Y.
B — V_X.
C — V_A.

17. How long does the Airworthiness Certificate of an aircraft remain valid?

A — As long as the aircraft has a current Registration Certificate.
B — Indefinitely, unless the aircraft suffers major damage.
C — As long as the aircraft is maintained and operated as required by Federal Aviation Regulations.

18. Except when necessary for takeoff or landing, what is the minimum safe altitude for a pilot to operate an aircraft anywhere?

A — An altitude allowing, if a power unit fails, an emergency landing without undue hazard to persons or property on the surface.
B — An altitude of 500 feet above the surface and no closer than 500 feet to any person, vessel, vehicle, or structure.
C — An altitude of 500 feet above the highest obstacle within a horizontal radius of 1,000 feet.

19. If an altimeter setting is not available before flight, to which altitude should the pilot adjust the altimeter?

A — The elevation of the nearest airport corrected to mean sea level.
B — The elevation of the departure area.
C — Pressure altitude corrected for nonstandard temperature.

20. What aircraft inspections are required for rental aircraft that are also used for flight instruction?

A — Annual and 100-hour inspections.
B — Biannual and 100-hour inspections.
C — Annual and 50-hour inspections.

21. What effect does high density altitude, as compared to low density altitude, have on propeller efficiency and why?

A — Efficiency is increased due to less friction on the propeller blades.
B — Efficiency is reduced because the propeller exerts less force at high density altitudes than at low density altitudes.
C — Efficiency is reduced due to the increased force of the propeller in the thinner air.

22. (Refer to figure 11 on page 74.) Determine the approximate ground roll distance required for takeoff.

OAT 100°F
Pressure altitude .... 2,000 ft
Takeoff weight .... 2,750 lb
Headwind component .... Calm

A — 1,150 feet.
B — 1,300 feet.
C — 1,800 feet.

23. (Refer to figure 5 on page 71.) Determine the total distance required to land over a 50-foot obstacle.

Pressure altitude .... 7,500 ft
Headwind .... 8 kts
Temperature .... 32°F
Runway .... Hard surface

A — 1,004 feet.
B — 1,205 feet.
C — 1,506 feet.

24. An aircraft is loaded 110 pounds over maximum certificated gross weight. If fuel (gasoline) is drained to bring the aircraft weight within limits, how much fuel should be drained?

A — 15.7 gallons.
B — 16.2 gallons.
C — 18.4 gallons.

25. (Refer to figure 16 on page 77.) Determine the aircraft loaded moment and the aircraft category.

	WEIGHT (LB)	MOM/1000
Empty weight	1,350	51.5
Pilot and front passenger	380	---
Fuel, 48 gal	288	---
Oil, 8 qt	---	---

A — 78.2, normal category.
B — 79.2, normal category.
C — 80.4, utility category.

STAGE TWO KNOWLEDGE TEST

The figures on the inside front and back covers and pages 71 through 80 are from the FAA's *Computerized Testing Supplement for Recreational Pilot and Private Pilot* book, which is available from your flight school or instructor.

1. Pilots are more subject to spatial disorientation if

A— they ignore the sensations of muscles and inner ear.
B— body signals are used to interpret flight attitude.
C— eyes are moved often in the process of cross-checking the flight instruments.

2. What is the most effective way to use the eyes during night flight?

A— Look only at far away, dim lights.
B— Scan slowly to permit offcenter viewing.
C— Concentrate directly on each object for a few seconds.

3. One weather phenomenon which will always occur when flying across a front is a change in the

A— wind direction.
B— type of precipitation.
C— stability of the air mass.

4. What conditions are necessary for the formation of thunderstorms?

A— High humidity, lifting force, and unstable conditions.
B— High humidity, high temperature, and cumulus clouds.
C— Lifting force, moist air, and extensive cloud cover.

5. When may hazardous wind shear be expected?

A— When stable air crosses a mountain barrier where it tends to flow in layers forming lenticular clouds.
B— In areas of low-level temperature inversion, frontal zones, and clear air turbulence.
C— Following frontal passage when stratocumulus clouds form indicating mechanical mixing.

6. Which conditions result in the formation of frost?

A— The temperature of the collecting surface is at or below freezing when small droplets of moisture fall on the surface.
B— The temperature of the collecting surface is at or below the dewpoint of the adjacent air and the dewpoint is below freezing.
C— The temperature of the surrounding air is at or below freezing when small drops of moisture fall on the collecting surface.

7. Steady precipitation preceding a front is an indication of

A— stratiform clouds with moderate turbulence.
B— cumuliform clouds with little or no turbulence.
C— stratiform clouds with little or no turbulence.

8. Which type weather briefing should a pilot request, when departing within the hour, if no preliminary weather information has been received?

A— Outlook briefing.
B— Abbreviated briefing.
C— Standard briefing.

9. (Refer to figure 9 on page 73.) The wind direction and velocity at KJFK is from

A— 180° true at 4 knots.
B— 180° magnetic at 4 knots.
C— 040° true at 18 knots.

10. (Refer to figure 8 on page 73.) In the TAF from KOKC, the clear sky becomes

A— overcast at 2,000 feet during the forecast period between 2200Z and 2400Z.
B— overcast at 200 feet with a 40% probability of becoming overcast at 600 feet during the forecast period between 2200Z and 2400Z.
C— overcast at 200 feet with the probability of becoming overcast at 400 feet during the forecast period between 2200Z and 2400Z.

11. What values are used for Winds Aloft Forecasts?

A— Magnetic direction and knots.
B— Magnetic direction and miles per hour.
C— True direction and knots.

12. What information is contained in a CONVECTIVE SIGMET?

A— Tornadoes, embedded thunderstorms, and hail 3/4 inch or greater in diameter.
B— Severe icing, severe turbulence, or widespread dust storms lowering visibility to less than 3 miles.
C— Surface winds greater than 40 knots or thunderstorms equal to or greater than video integrator processor (VIP) level 4.

13. (Refer to figure 20 on the inside front cover, area 1.) Determine the approximate longitude of Allendale County Airport.

A— 81° 17'N
B— 81° 17'W
C— 80° 43'W

14. (Refer to figure 21 on the inside back cover, area 9.) Identify the airspace over Mesquite Airport that exists from the surface to 11,000 feet MSL.

A — Class G airspace -- surface to 700 feet AGL; Class E airspace -- 700 feet AGL to 4,000 feet MSL; Class B airspace -- 4,000 feet MSL to 11,000 feet MSL.

B — Class G airspace -- surface to 4,000 feet MSL; Class B airspace -- 4,000 feet MSL to 11,000 feet MSL.

C — Class G airspace -- surface to 1,200 feet AGL; Class E airspace -- 1,200 feet AGL to 11,000 feet MSL.

15. (Refer to figure 20 on the inside front cover, area 1.) Which public use airport has fuel available?

A — Allendale County Airport.
B — Broxton Bridge Airport.
C — Hampton Varnville Airport.

16. (Refer to figure 21 on the inside back cover, area 9.) What is the recommended communications procedure for a landing at Mesquite Airport?

A — Transmit intentions on 123.05 MHz when 10 miles out and give position reports in the traffic pattern.

B — Contact Dallas-Ft. Worth approach for a landing clearance.

C — Contact Ft. Worth FSS on 122.3 MHz for area traffic information.

17. (Refer to figure 13 on page 75.) Traffic patterns in effect at Lincoln Municipal are

A — to the right on Runway 17L and Runway 35L; to the left on Runway 17R and Runway 35R.

B — to the left on Runway 17L and Runway 35L; to the right on Runway 17R and Runway 35R.

C — to the right on Runways 14 - 32.

18. When the course deviation indicator (CDI) needle is centered during an omnireceiver check using a VOR test signal (VOT), the omnibearing selector (OBS) and the TO/FROM indicator should read

A — 180° FROM, only if the pilot is due north of the VOT.

B — 0° TO or 180° FROM, regardless of the pilot's position from the VOT.

C — 0° FROM or 180° TO, regardless of the pilot's position from the VOT.

19. (Refer to figure 20 on the inside front cover.) What is the approximate position of the aircraft if the VOR receivers indicate the 320° radial of Savannah VORTAC (area 3) and the 184° radial of Allendale VOR (area 1)?

A — Town of Springfield.
B — Town of Guyton.
C — 3 miles east of Marlow.

20. (Refer to figure 15, illustration 1, on page 76.) The VOR receiver has the indications shown. What is the aircraft's position relative to the station?

A — North.
B — South.
C — East.

21. (Refer to figure 14 on page 75.) What information should be entered in block 9 for a VFR day flight?

A — The name of the airport of first intended landing.

B — The name of destination airport if no stopover for more than 1 hour is anticipated.

C — The name of the airport where the aircraft is based.

22. (Refer to figure 20 on the inside front cover.) Determine the magnetic course from Ridgeland Airport (area 3) to Claxton-Evans County Airport (area 2).

A — 73°.
B — 243°.
C — 253°.

23. (Refer to figure 21 on the inside back cover.) Determine the magnetic heading for a flight from Fort Worth Meacham (area 4) to Denton Muni (area 1). The wind is from 330° at 25 knots, the true airspeed is 110 knots, and the magnetic variation is 7° east.

A — 003°.
B — 017°.
C — 023°.

24. (Refer to figure 20 on the inside front cover.) Determine the magnetic heading for a flight from Claxton-Evans County Airport (area 2) to Hampton Varnville Airport (area 1). The wind is from 290° at 18 knots and the true airspeed is 85 knots.

A — 039°.
B — 033°.
C — 049°.

25. (Refer to figure 21 on the inside back cover.) What is the estimated time en route for a flight from Denton Muni (area 1) to Addison (area 2)? The wind is from 200° at 20 knots, the true airspeed is 110 knots, and the magnetic variation is 7° east.

A — 13 minutes.
B — 16 minutes.
C — 19 minutes.

END-OF-COURSE KNOWLEDGE TEST

The figures on the inside front and back covers and pages 71 through 80 are from the FAA's *Computerized Testing Supplement for Recreational Pilot and Private Pilot* book, which is available from your flight school or instructor.

1. With respect to the certification of airmen, which are categories of aircraft?

A— Gyroplane, helicopter, airship, free balloon.
B— Airplane, rotorcraft, glider, lighter-than-air.
C— Single-engine land and sea, multiengine land and sea.

2. When must a current pilot certificate be in the pilot's personal possession or readily accessible in the aircraft?

A— When acting as a crew chief during launch and recovery.
B— Only when passengers are carried.
C— Anytime when acting as pilot in command or as a required crewmember.

3. The three takeoffs and landings that are required to act as pilot in command at night must be done during the time period from

A— sunset to sunrise.
B— 1 hour after sunset to 1 hour before sunrise.
C— the end of evening civil twilight to the beginning of morning civil twilight.

4. In regard to privileges and limitations, a private pilot may

A— act as pilot in command of an aircraft carrying a passenger for compensation if the flight is in connection with a business or employment.
B— not pay less than the pro rata share of the operating expenses of a flight with passengers provided the expenses involve only fuel, oil, airport expenditures, or rental fees.
C— not be paid in any manner for the operating expenses of a flight.

5. Under what condition, if any, may a pilot allow a person who is obviously under the influence of drugs to be carried aboard an aircraft?

A— In an emergency or if the person is a medical patient under proper care.
B— Only if the person does not have access to the cockpit or pilot's compartment.
C— Under no condition.

6. An airplane and an airship are converging. If the airship is left of the airplane's position, which aircraft has the right-of-way?

A— The airship.
B— The airplane.
C— Each pilot should alter course to the right.

7. Prior to takeoff, the altimeter should be set to which altitude or altimeter setting?

A— The current local altimeter setting, if available, or the departure airport elevation.
B— The corrected density altitude of the departure airport.
C— The corrected pressure altitude for the departure airport.

8. Each pilot of an aircraft approaching to land on a runway served by a visual approach slope indicator (VASI) shall

A— maintain a 3° glide to the runway.
B— maintain an altitude at or above the glide slope.
C— stay high until the runway can be reached in a power-off landing.

9. During operations within controlled airspace at altitudes of less than 1,200 feet AGL, the minimum horizontal distance from clouds requirement for VFR flight is

A— 1,000 feet.
B— 1,500 feet.
C— 2,000 feet.

10. Unless each occupant is provided with supplemental oxygen, no person may operate a civil aircraft of U.S. registry above a maximum cabin pressure altitude of

A— 12,500 feet MSL.
B— 14,000 feet MSL.
C— 15,000 feet MSL.

11. A 100-hour inspection was due at 3302.5 hours on the tachometer. The 100-hour inspection was actually done at 3309.5 hours. When is the next 100-hour inspection due?

A— 3312.5 hours.
B— 3402.5 hours.
C— 3409.5 hours.

12. Which incident requires an immediate notification be made to the nearest NTSB field office?

A— An overdue aircraft that is believed to be involved in an accident.
B— An in-flight radio communications failure.
C— An in-flight generator or alternator failure.

13. When are the four forces that act on an airplane in equilibrium?

A— During unaccelerated flight.
B— When the aircraft is accelerating.
C— When the aircraft is at rest on the ground.

14. What determines the longitudinal stability of an airplane?

A— The location of the CG with respect to the center of lift.
B— The effectiveness of the horizontal stabilizer, rudder, and rudder trim tab.
C— The relationship of thrust and lift to weight and drag.

15. What is one purpose of wing flaps?

A— To enable the pilot to make steeper approaches to a landing without increasing the airspeed.
B— To relieve the pilot of maintaining continuous pressure on the controls.
C— To decrease wing area to vary the lift.

16. Which condition is most favorable to the development of carburetor icing?

A— Any temperature below freezing and a relative humidity of less than 50 percent.
B— Temperature between 32 and 50°F and low humidity.
C— Temperature between 20 and 70°F and high humidity.

17. Detonation occurs in a reciprocating aircraft engine when

A— the spark plugs are fouled or shorted out or the wiring is defective.
B— hot spots in the combustion chamber ignite the fuel/air mixture in advance of normal ignition.
C— the unburned charge in the cylinders explodes instead of burning normally.

18. If the pitot tube and outside static vents become clogged, which instruments would be affected?

A— The altimeter, airspeed indicator, and turn-and-slip indicator.
B— The altimeter, airspeed indicator, and vertical speed indicator.
C— The altimeter, attitude indicator, and turn-and-slip indicator.

19. What is true altitude?

A— The vertical distance of the aircraft above sea level.
B— The vertical distance of the aircraft above the surface.
C— The height above the standard datum plane.

20. (Refer to figure 1 on page 71.) What is the full flap operating range for the airplane?

A— 60 to 100 MPH.
B— 60 to 208 MPH.
C— 65 to 165 MPH.

21. What is an important airspeed limitation that is not color coded on airspeed indicators?

A— Never-exceed speed.
B— Maximum structural cruising speed.
C— Maneuvering speed.

22. In the Northern Hemisphere, the magnetic compass will normally indicate a turn toward the south when

A— a left turn is entered from an east heading.
B— a right turn is entered from a west heading.
C— the aircraft is decelerated while on a west heading.

23. (Refer to figure 6 on page 72.) What is the effect of a temperature increase from 25 to 50°F on the density altitude if the pressure altitude remains at 5,000 feet?

A— 1,200-foot increase.
B— 1,400-foot increase.
C— 1,650-foot increase.

24. (Refer to figure 2 on page 71, area C.) How should the flight controls be held while taxiing a tailwheel airplane with a left quartering tailwind?

A— Left aileron up, elevator neutral.
B— Left aileron down, elevator neutral.
C— Left aileron down, elevator down.

25. Every physical process of weather is accompanied by, or is the result of, a

A— movement of air.
B— pressure differential.
C— heat exchange.

26. Which condition would cause the altimeter to indicate a lower altitude than true altitude?

A— Air temperature lower than standard.
B— Atmospheric pressure lower than standard.
C— Air temperature warmer than standard.

27. The presence of ice pellets at the surface is evidence that there

A— are thunderstorms in the area.
B— has been cold frontal passage.
C— is a temperature inversion with freezing rain at a higher altitude.

28. A stable air mass is most likely to have which characteristic?

A — Showery precipitation.
B — Turbulent air.
C — Smooth air.

29. Where does wind shear occur?

A — Only at higher altitudes.
B — Only at lower altitudes.
C — At all altitudes, in all directions.

30. Thunderstorms reach their greatest intensity during the

A — mature stage.
B — downdraft stage.
C — cumulus stage.

31. Convective circulation patterns associated with sea breezes are caused by

A — warm, dense air moving inland from over the water.
B — water absorbing and radiating heat faster than the land.
C — cool, dense air moving inland from over the water.

32. (Refer to figure 9 on page 73.) Which of the reporting stations have VFR weather?

A — All.
B — KINK, KBOI, and KJFK.
C — KINK, KBOI, and KLAX.

33. (Refer to figure 7 on page 72.) If the terrain elevation is 1,295 feet MSL, what is the height above ground level of the base of the ceiling?

A — 505 feet AGL.
B — 1,295 feet AGL.
C — 6,586 feet AGL.

34. (Refer to figure 8 on page 73.) The only cloud type forecast in TAF reports is

A — Nimbostratus.
B — Cumulonimbus.
C — Scattered cumulus.

35. Which in-flight advisory would contain information on severe icing not associated with thunderstorms?

A — Convective SIGMET.
B — SIGMET.
C — AIRMET.

36. (Refer to figure 19, area B, on page 80.) What is the top for precipitation of the radar return?

A — 24,000 feet AGL.
B — 24,000 feet MSL.
C — 2,400 feet MSL.

37. (Refer to figure 20 on the inside front cover, area 2.) Determine the approximate longitude of Statesboro-Bulloch County Airport.

A — 81° 44'W.
B — 80° 16'E.
C — 181° 44'W.

38. (Refer to figure 20 on the inside front cover.) What course should be selected on the omnibearing selector (OBS) to make a direct flight from Claxton-Evans County Airport (area 2) to the Allendale VOR (area 1) with a TO indication?

A — 032°.
B — 212°.
C — 94°.

39. (Refer to figure 20 on the inside front cover.) What is the estimated time en route for a flight from Claxton-Evans County Airport (area 2) to Hampton Varnville Airport (area 1)? The wind is from 290° at 18 knots and the true airspeed is 85 knots. Add 2 minutes for climb-out.

A — 35 minutes.
B — 39 minutes.
C — 44 minutes.

40. (Refer to figure 20 on the inside front cover.) What is the approximate position of the aircraft if the VOR receivers indicate the 216° radial of Allendale VOR (area 1) and the 303° radial of Savannah VORTAC (area 3)?

A — 4 NM east of Bulloch County NDB.
B — Statesboro-Bulloch County Airport.
C — DOVER intersection.

41. (Refer to figure 20 on the inside front cover, area 1.) Determine the magnetic course from Hampton Varnville Airport to Allendale County Airport.

A — 307°.
B — 302°.
C — 312°.

42. (Refer to figure 15, illustration 3, on page 76.) The VOR receiver has the indications shown. What is the aircraft's position relative to the station?

A — East.
B — Southeast.
C — West.

43. (Refer to figure 15 on page 76, illustration 6.) While tracing to the station on the 030° radial, you observe the following VOR indications. Your aircraft is

A — left of course and southwest of the station.
B — left of course and northeast of the station.
C — right of course and northeast of the station.

44. (Refer to figure 21 on the inside back cover, area 2.) The floor of Class B airspace at Addison Airport is

A — at the surface.
B — 3,000 feet MSL.
C — 3,100 feet MSL.

45. (Refer to figure 20 on the inside front cover, area 1.) What is the recommended communication procedure when inbound to land at Hampton Varnville Airport?

A — Broadcast intentions when 10 miles out on the CTAF/MULTICOM frequency, 122.9 MHz.
B — Contact UNICOM when 10 miles out on 122.8 MHz.
C — Circle the airport in a left turn prior to entering traffic.

46. (Refer to figure 21 on the inside back cover, area 4.) The airspace directly overlying Fort Worth Meacham is

A — Class B airspace to 10,000 feet MSL.
B — Class C airspace to 5,000 feet MSL.
C — Class D airspace to 3,200 feet MSL.

47. (Refer to figure 20 on the inside front cover, area 3.) What is the height of the lighted obstacle approximately 6 nautical miles southwest of Savannah International?

A — 1,500 feet MSL.
B — 1,531 feet AGL.
C — 1,549 feet MSL.

48. (Refer to figure 21 on the inside back cover, area 2.) The control tower frequency for Addison Airport is

A — 122.95 MHz.
B — 126.0 MHz.
C — 133.4 MHz.

49. What action can a pilot take to aid in cooling an engine that is overheating during a climb?

A — Reduce rate of climb and increase airspeed.
B — Reduce climb speed and increase RPM.
C — Increase climb speed and increase RPM.

50. If an aircraft is loaded 90 pounds over maximum certificated gross weight and fuel (gasoline) is drained to bring the aircraft weight within limits, how much fuel should be drained?

A — 10 gallons.
B — 12 gallons.
C — 15 gallons.

51. (Refer to figures 17 and 18 on pages 78 and 79.) Which action can adjust the airplane's weight to maximum gross weight and the CG within limits for takeoff?

Front seat occupants	425 lb
Rear seat occupants	300 lb
Fuel, main tanks	44 gal

A — Drain 12 gallons of fuel.
B — Drain 9 gallons of fuel.
C — Transfer 12 gallons of fuel from the main tanks to the auxiliary tanks.

52. (Refer to figure 10 on page 73.) With a reported wind of south at 20 knots, which runway (10, 14, or 24) is appropriate for an airplane with a 13-knot maximum crosswind component?

A — Runway 10.
B — Runway 14.
C — Runway 24.

53. (Refer to figure 11 on page 74.) Determine the total distance required for takeoff to clear a 50-foot obstacle.

OAT Std	
Pressure altitude	4,000 ft
Takeoff weight	2,800 lb
Headwind component	Calm

A — 1,500 feet
B — 1,750 feet.
C — 2,000 feet.

54. Prior to starting each maneuver, pilots should

A — check altitude, airspeed, and heading indications.
B — visually scan the entire area for collision avoidance.
C — announce their intentions on the nearest CTAF.

55. During a night flight, you observe a steady red light and a flashing red light ahead and at the same altitude. What is the general direction of movement of the other aircraft?

A — The other aircraft is crossing to the left.
B — The other aircraft is crossing to the right.
C — The other aircraft is approaching head-on.

56. VFR approaches to land at night should be accomplished

A — at a higher airspeed.
B — with a steeper descent.
C — the same as during daytime.

57. (Refer to figure 4 on page 71.) Illustration A indicates that the aircraft is

A — below the glide slope.
B — on the glide slope.
C — above the glide slope.

58. Prior to entering an Airport Advisory Area, a pilot should

A — monitor ATIS for weather and traffic advisories.
B — contact approach control for vectors to the traffic pattern.
C — contact the local FSS for airport and traffic advisories.

59. What ATC facility should the pilot contact to receive a special VFR departure clearance in Class D airspace?

A — Automated Flight Service Station.
B — Air Traffic Control Tower.
C — Air Route Traffic Control Center.

60. Which statement best defines hypoxia?

A — A state of oxygen deficiency in the body.
B — An abnormal increase in the volume of air breathed.
C — A condition of gas bubble formation around the joints or muscles.

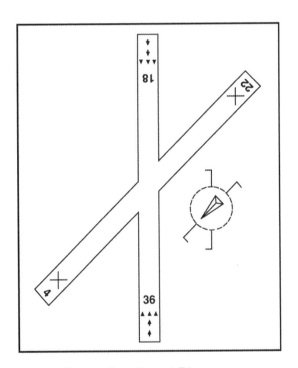

Figure 1.—Airspeed Indicator.

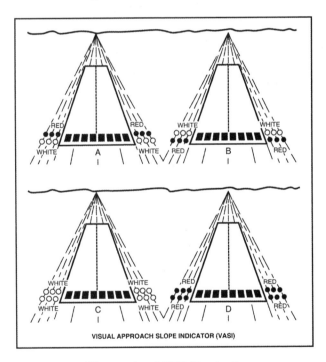

Figure 2.—Control Position for Taxi.

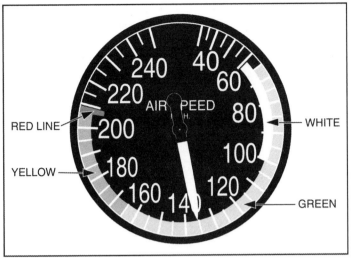

Figure 3.—Airport Diagram.

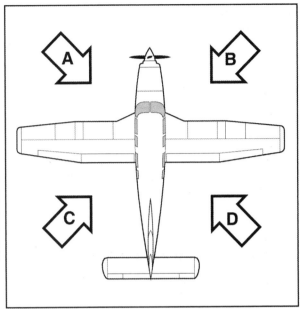

Figure 4.—VASI Illustrations.

GROSS WEIGHT LB	APPROACH SPEED, IAS, MPH	AT SEA LEVEL & 59° F		AT 2500 FT & 50° F		AT 5000 FT & 41° F		AT 7500 FT & 32° F	
		GROUND ROLL	TOTAL TO CLEAR 50 FT OBS	GROUND ROLL	TOTAL TO CLEAR 50 FT OBS	GROUND ROLL	TOTAL TO CLEAR 50 FT OBS	GROUND ROLL	TOTAL TO CLEAR 50 FT OBS
1600	60	445	1075	470	1135	495	1195	520	1255

LANDING DISTANCE — FLAPS LOWERED TO 40 ° - POWER OFF — HARD SURFACE RUNWAY - ZERO WIND

NOTES: 1. Decrease the distances shown by 10% for each 4 knots of headwind.
2. Increase the distance by 10% for each 60° F temperature increase above standard.
3. For operation on a dry, grass runway, increase distances (both "ground roll" and "total to clear 50 ft obstacle") by 20% of the "total to clear 50 ft obstacle" figure.

Figure 5.—Airplane Landing Distance Table.

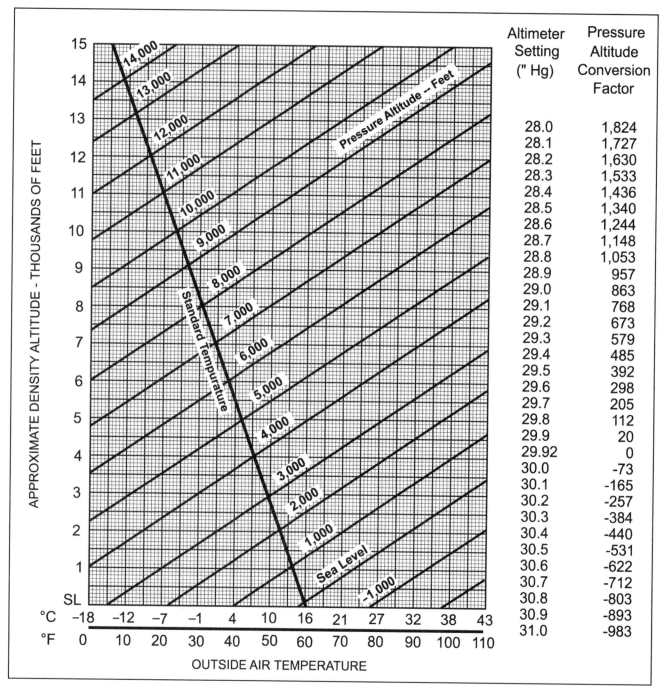

Figure 6.—Density Altitude Chart.

UA/OV KOKC-KTUL/TM 1800/FL120/TP BE90//SK BKN018-TOP055/OVC072-
TOP089/CLR ABV/TA M7/WV 08021/TB LGT 055-072/IC LGT-MOD RIME 072-089

Figure 7.—Pilot Weather Report.

TAF

KMEM   121720Z 121818 20012KT 5SM HZ BKN030 PROB40 2022 1SM TSRA OVC008CB
        FM2200 33015G20KT P6SM BKN015 OVC025 PROB40 2202 3SM SHRA
        FM0200 35012KT OVC008 PROB40 0205 2SM -RASN BECMG 0608 02008KT BKN012
         BECMG 1012 00000KT 3SM BR SKC TEMPO 1214 1/2SM FG
        FM1600 VRB06KT P6SM SKC=

KOKC   051130Z 051212 14008KT 5SM BR BKN030 TEMPO 1316 1 1/2SM BR
        FM1600 18010KT P6SM SKC BECMG 2224 20013G20KT 4SM SHRA OVC020
        PROB40 0006 2SM TSRA OVC008CB BECMG 0608 21015KT P6SM SCT040=

Figure 8.—Terminal Aerodrome Forecasts (TAF).

METAR KINK 121845Z 11012G18KT 15SM SKC 25/17 A3000

METAR KBOI 121854Z 13004KT 30SM SCT150 17/6 A3015

METAR KLAX 121852Z 25004KT 6SM BR SCT007 SCT250 16/15 A2991

**SPECI KMDW 121856Z 32005KT 1 1/2SM RA OVC007 17/16 A2980 RMK
RAB35**

SPECI KJFK 121853Z 18004KT 1/2SM FG R04/2200 OVC005 20/18 A3006

Figure 9.—Aviation Routine Weather Reports (METAR).

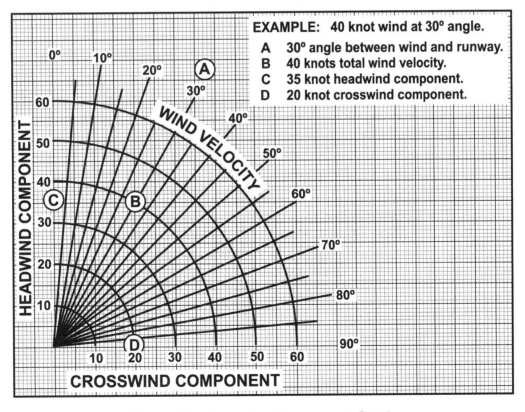

Figure 10.—Crosswind Component Graph.

TAKEOFF DISTANCE

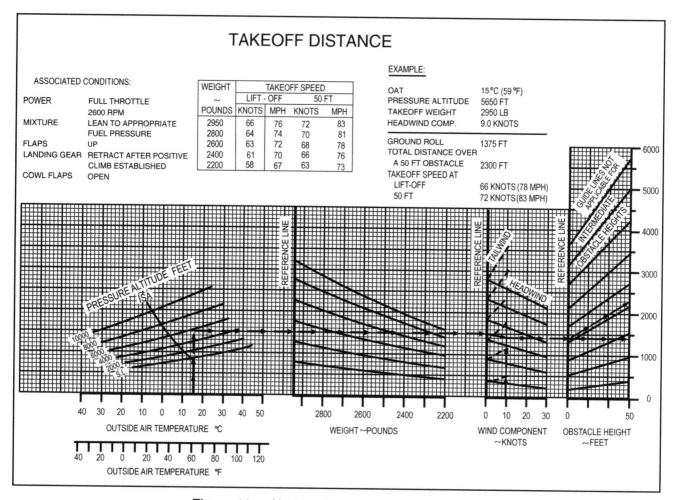

ASSOCIATED CONDITIONS:

POWER	FULL THROTTLE
	2600 RPM
MIXTURE	LEAN TO APPROPRIATE
	FUEL PRESSURE
FLAPS	UP
LANDING GEAR	RETRACT AFTER POSITIVE
	CLIMB ESTABLISHED
COWL FLAPS	OPEN

WEIGHT ~ POUNDS	TAKEOFF SPEED			
	LIFT - OFF		50 FT	
	KNOTS	MPH	KNOTS	MPH
2950	66	76	72	83
2800	64	74	70	81
2600	63	72	68	78
2400	61	70	66	76
2200	58	67	63	73

EXAMPLE:

OAT	15 °C (59 °F)
PRESSURE ALTITUDE	5650 FT
TAKEOFF WEIGHT	2950 LB
HEADWIND COMP.	9.0 KNOTS
GROUND ROLL	1375 FT
TOTAL DISTANCE OVER A 50 FT OBSTACLE	2300 FT
TAKEOFF SPEED AT	
LIFT-OFF	66 KNOTS (78 MPH)
50 FT	72 KNOTS (83 MPH)

Figure 11.—Airplane Takeoff Distance Graph.

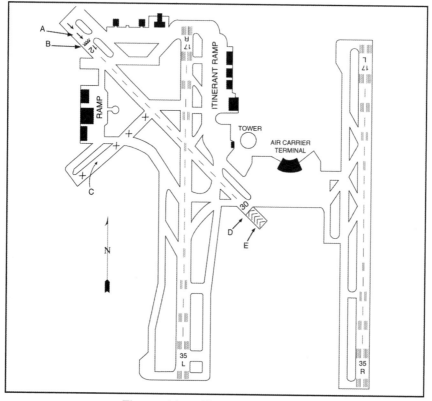

Figure 12.—Airport Diagram.

```
180                              NEBRASKA
```

LINCOLN MUNI (LNK)   4 NW   UTC–6(–5DT)   N40°-51.05' W98°-45.55'   **OMAHA**
  1218   B   S4   **FUEL** 100LL. JET A   TPA—2218(1000)   ARFF Index B   H–1E, 3F, 4F, L–11B
  RWY 17R–35L: H129001X200 (ASPH–CONC–GRVD)   S–100. D–200. DT–400   HIRL   **IAP**
    RWY 17R: MALSR. VASI(V4L)—GA 3.0°TCH 55'. Rgt tfc.   0.4% down.
    RWY 35L: MALSR. VASI(V4L)—GA 3.0°TCH 55'.
  RWY 14–-32: H8620X150 (ASPH–CONC–GRVD)   S–80. D–170. DT–280   MIRL
    RWY 14: REIL. VASI(V4L)—GA 3.0°TCH 48'.
    RWY 32: VASI(V4L)—GA 3.0° TCH 53'. Thld dsplcd 431'. Pole.   0.3% up.
  RWY 17R–35R: H5400X100 (ASPH–CONC–AFSC)   S–49. D–60   HIRL   0.8% up N
    RWY 17L: PAPI(P4L)—GA 3.0° TCH 33'.   **RWY 35R** PAPI(P4L)—GA 3.0°TCH 40'. Pole. Rgt tfc.
  AIRPORT REMARKS: Attended continuously. Birds in vicinity of arpt. Twy D clsd between taxiways S and H indef. For
    MALSR Rwy 17R and Rwy 35L ctc twr. When twr clsd MALSR Rwy 17R and Rwy 35l preset on med ints. and REIL
    Rwy 14 left on when wind favor,NOTE: See Land and Hold Short Operations Section.
  WEATHER DATA SOURCES: ASOS (1402) 474-9214. LLWAS
  COMMUNICATIONS: CTAF 118.5   **ATIS** 118.05   **UNICOM** 122.95
    COLUMBUS FSS (OLU) TF 1–800–WX–BRIEF. NOTAM FILE LNK.
    RCO 122.65 (COLUMBUS FSS)
  ® APP/DEP CON 124.0 (170°–349°) 124.8 (350°–169°) (1130–0630Z‡)
  ® MINNEAPOLIS CENTER APP/DEP CON 128.75 (0630–1130Z‡)
    TOWER 118.5 125.7(1130–0630Z‡)   GND CON 121.9   CLNC DEL 120.7
  AIRSPACE: CLASS C svc (1130–0630Z‡ctc **APP CON** other times CLASS E.
  RADIO AIDS TO NAVIGATION: NOTAM FILE LNK. VHF/DF ctc FSS.
    (H) VORTACW 116.1   LNK   Chan 108   N40°55.43' W 96°44.52'   181° 4.5 NM to fld. 1370/9E
    POTTS NDB (MHW/LOM) 385   LN   N40°44.83' W 96°45.75'   355° 6.2 NM to fld. Unmonitored when twr clsd.
    ILS 111.1   I–OCZ   Rwy 17R.   MM and OM unmonitored
    ILS 109.9   I–LNK   Rwy 35L.   LOM POTTS NDB.MM unmonitored LOM unmonitored when twr clsd.
  COMM/NAVAID REMARKS: Emerg frequency 121.5 not available at tower.

Figure 13.—Airport/Facility Directory Excerpt.

					Form Approved: OMB No. 2120-0034
U.S. DEPARTMENT OF TRANSPORTATION FEDERAL AVIATION ADMINISTRATION **FLIGHT PLAN**	(FAA USE ONLY) ☐ PILOT BRIEFING ☐ STOPOVER	☐ VNR	TIME STARTED		SPECIALIST INITIALS

1. TYPE	2. AIRCRAFT IDENTIFICATION	3. AIRCRAFT TYPE/ SPECIAL EQUIPMENT	4. TRUE AIRSPEED	5. DEPARTURE POINT	6. DEPARTURE TIME		7. CRUISING ALTITUDE
VFR IFR DVFR			KTS		PROPOSED (Z)	ACTUAL (Z)	

8. ROUTE OF FLIGHT

9. DESTINATION (Name of airport and city)	10. EST. TIME ENROUTE		11. REMARKS
	HOURS	MINUTES	

12. FUEL ON BOARD		13. ALTERNATE AIRPORT(S)	14. PILOTS NAME, ADDRESS & TELEPHONE NUMBER & AIRCRAFT HOME BASE	15. NUMBER ABOARD
HOURS	MINUTES		17. DESTINATION CONTACT/TELEPHONE (OPTIONAL)	

16. COLOR OF AIRCRAFT	CIVIL AIRCRAFT PILOTS. FAR Part 91 requires you file an IFR flight plan to operate under instrument flight rules in controlled airspace. Failure to file could result in a civil penalty not to exceed $1,000 for each violation (Section 901 of the Federal Aviation Act of 1958, as amended). Filing of a VFR flight plan is recommended as a good operating practice. See also Part 99 for requirements concerning DVFR flight plans.

FAA Form 7233-1 (8-82)   CLOSE VFR FLIGHT PLAN WITH _____ FSS ON ARRIVAL

Figure 14.—Flight Plan Form.

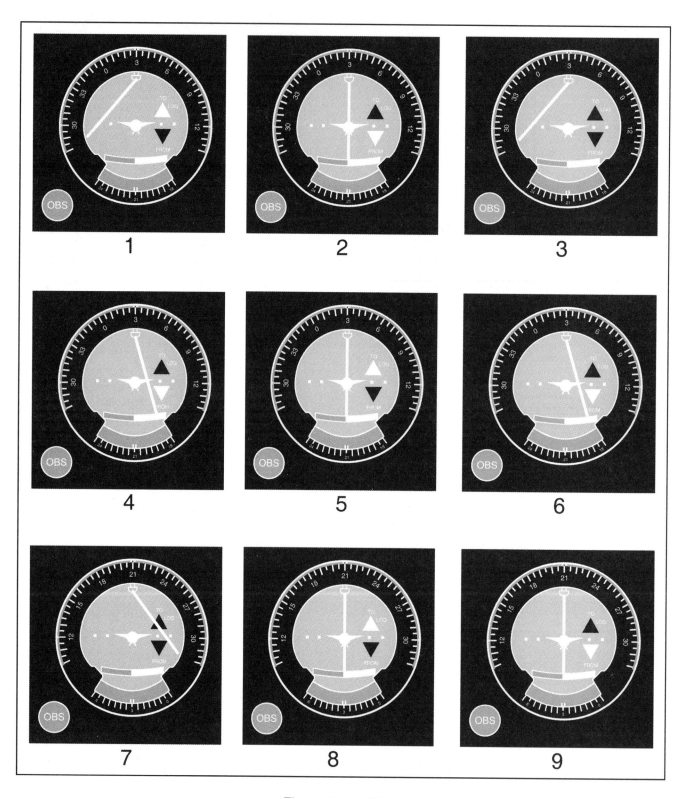

Figure 15.—VOR.

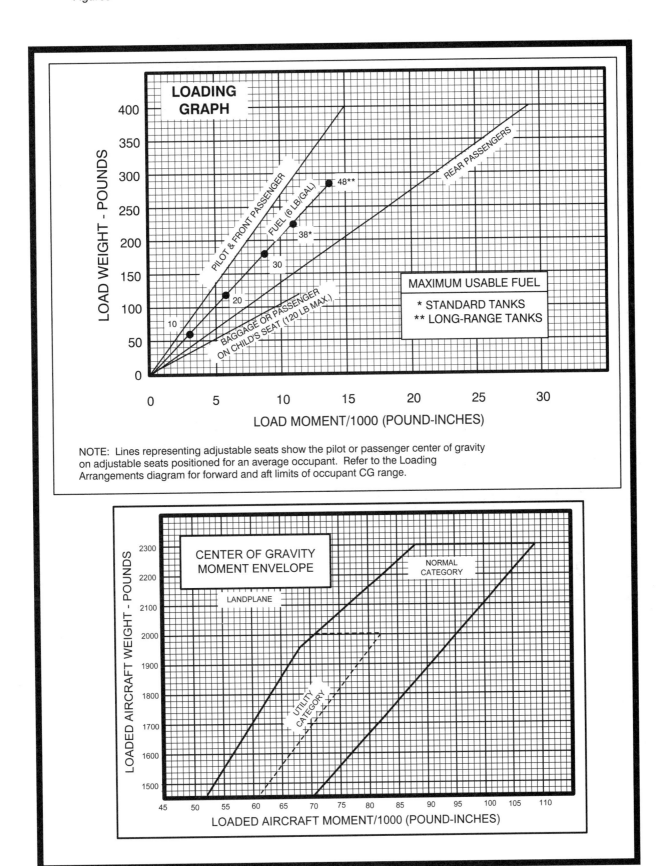

Figure 16.—Airplane Weight and Balance Graphs.

MOMENTS LIMITS vs WEIGHT (Continued)

Weight	Minimum Moment 100	Maximum Moment 100
2100	1617	1800
2110	1625	1808
2120	1632	1817
2130	1640	1825
2140	1648	1834
2150	1656	1843
2160	1663	1851
2170	1671	1860
2180	1679	1868
2190	1686	1877
2200	1694	1885
2210	1702	1894
2220	1709	1903
2230	1717	1911
2240	1725	1920
2250	1733	1928
2260	1740	1937
2270	1748	1945
2280	1756	1954
2290	1763	1963
2300	1771	1971
2310	1779	1980
2320	1786	1988
2330	1794	1997
2340	1802	2005
2350	1810	2014
2360	1817	2023
2370	1825	2031
2380	1833	2040
2390	1840	2048
2400	1848	2057
2410	1856	2065
2420	1863	2074
2430	1871	2083
2440	1879	2091
2450	1887	2100
2460	1894	2108
2470	1902	2117
2480	1911	2125
2490	1921	2134
2500	1932	2143
2510	1942	2151
2520	1953	2160
2530	1963	2168
2540	1974	2176
2550	1984	2184
2560	1995	2192
2570	2005	2200
2580	2016	2208
2590	2026	2216

Weight	Minimum Moment 100	Maximum Moment 100
2600	2037	2224
2610	2048	2232
2620	2058	2239
2630	2069	2247
2640	2080	2255
2650	2090	2263
2660	2101	2271
2670	2112	2279
2680	2123	2287
2690	2133	2295
2700	2144	2303
2710	2155	2311
2720	2166	2319
2730	2177	2326
2740	2188	2334
2750	2199	2342
2760	2210	2350
2770	2221	2358
2780	2232	2366
2790	2243	2374
2800	2254	2381
2810	2265	2389
2820	2276	2397
2830	2287	2405
2840	2298	2413
2850	2309	2421
2860	2320	2428
2870	2332	2436
2880	2343	2444
2890	2354	2452
2900	2365	2460
2910	2377	2468
2920	2388	2475
2930	2399	2483
2940	2411	2491
2950	2422	2499

Figure 17.—Airplane Weight and Balance Tables.

USEFUL LOAD WEIGHTS AND MOMENTS

OCCUPANTS

FRONT SEATS ARM 85		REAR SEATS ARM 121	
Weight	Moment 100	Weight	Moment 100
120	102	120	145
130	110	130	157
140	119	140	169
150	128	150	182
160	136	160	194
170	144	170	206
180	153	180	218
190	162	190	230
200	170	200	242

USABLE FUEL

MAIN WING TANKS ARM 75

Gallons	Weight	Moment 100
5	30	22
10	60	45
15	90	68
20	120	90
25	150	112
30	180	135
35	210	158
40	240	180
44	264	198

BAGGAGE OR 5TH SEAT OCCUPANT ARM 140

Weight	Moment 100
10	14
20	28
30	42
40	56
50	70
60	84
70	98
80	112
90	126
100	140
110	154
120	168
130	182
140	196
150	210
160	224
170	238
180	252
190	266
200	280
210	294
220	308
230	322
240	336
250	350
260	364
270	378

AUXILIARY WING TANKS ARM 94

Gallons	Weight	Moment 100
5	30	28
10	60	56
15	90	85
19	114	107

*OIL

Quarts	Weight	Moment 100
10	19	5

*Included in basic Empty Weight

Empty Weight ~ 2015
MOM/ 100 ~ 1554

MOMENT LIMITS vs WEIGHT

Moment limits are based on the following weight and center of gravity limit data (landing gear down).

Weight Condition	Forward CG Limit	AFT CG Limit
2950 lb (takeoff or landing)	82.1	84.7
2525 lb	77.5	85.7
2475 lb or less	77.0	85.7

Figure 18.—Airplane Weight and Balance Tables.

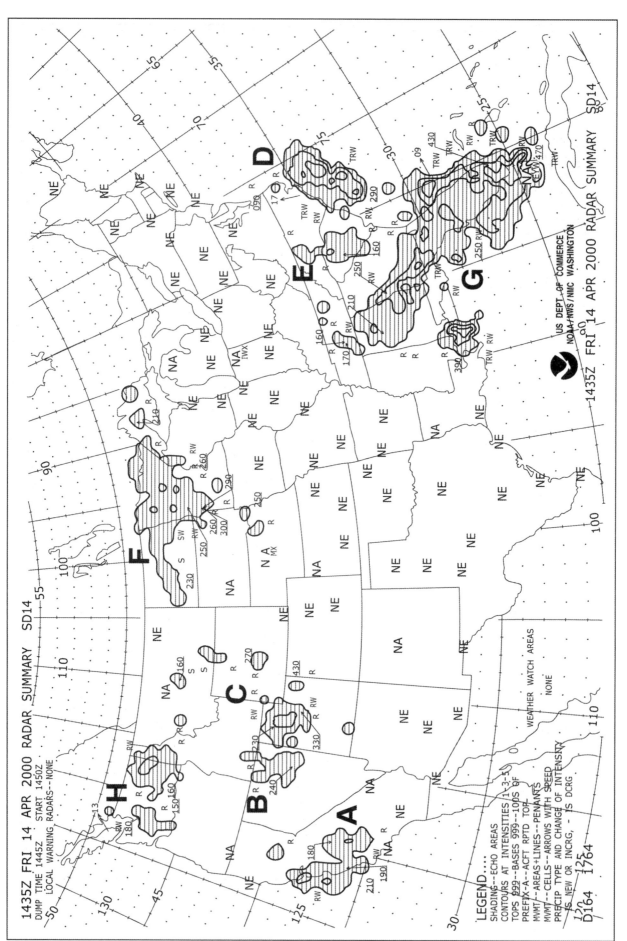

Figure 19.—Radar Summary Chart.

This is to certify that

_____

is enrolled in the

Federal Aviation Administration

approved Private Pilot Certification Course

conducted by _____ .

(name of school and certificate number)

_____
Chief Instructor

_____
Date of Enrollment

Gleim Publications, Inc.
P.O. Box 12848,
University Station
Gainesville, Florida 32604
(800) 87-GLEIM
(352) 375-0772
(352) 375-6940 FAX
Internet: www.gleim.com
E-Mail: admin@gleim.com

This is to certify that

_____

has satisfactorily completed all stages, tests, and course requirements and has graduated from the **FEDERAL AVIATION ADMINISTRATION** approved Private Pilot Certification Course

conducted by _____
(name of school and certificate number)

The graduate has received _____ hours of cross-country training.

_____
Date of Graduation

_____
Chief Instructor

Gleim Publications, Inc.
P.O. Box 12848,
University Station
Gainesville, Florida 32604
(800) 87-GLEIM
(352) 375-0772
(352) 375-6940 FAX
Internet: www.gleim.com
E-Mail: admin@gleim.com

INTRODUCTORY FLIGHT LOG SHEET

If you take one or more introductory flights to help you select the flight school at which you will be most comfortable, have the CFI record your flight time below. If you already have a logbook, be sure to have your CFI record the flight time in it and sign the entry as well.

1.   Date: _____ Airplane Make and Model: _____N-number:

       To/From: _____ Total Flight Training Time:

       Comments:

_____ _____

CFI Signature   CFI Cert. No.   Exp. Date

2.   Date: _____ Airplane Make and Model: _____N-number:

       To/From: _____ Total Flight Training Time:

       Comments:

_____ _____

CFI Signature   CFI Cert. No.   Exp. Date

3.   Date: _____ Airplane Make and Model: _____N-number:

       To/From: _____ Total Flight Training Time:

       Comments:

_____ _____

CFI Signature   CFI Cert. No.   Exp. Date

The online FAA MedXPress system allows you to complete Form 8500-8 electronically. Your information will be transmitted to the FAA and will be available for your AME to review at the time of your medical examination. Go to https://medxpress.faa.gov. Alternatively, you can complete items 1 through 20 when you arrive at your AME's office. Review the items now to be sure you can complete the information when the time comes.

Instructions for Completion of the Application for Airman Medical Certificate or Airman Medical and Student Pilot Certificate, FAA Form 8500-8

Applicant must fill in completely numbers 1 through 20 of the application using a ballpoint pen. Exert sufficient pressure to make legible copies. The following numbered instructions apply to the numbered headings on the application form that follows this page.

NOTICE – Intentional falsification may result in federal criminal prosecution. Intentional falsification may also result in suspension or revocation of all airman, ground instructor, and medical certificates and ratings held by you, as well as denial of this application for medical certification.

1. APPLICATION FOR -- Check the appropriate box.

2. CLASS OF AIRMAN MEDICAL CERTIFICATE APPLIED FOR -- Check the appropriate box for the class of airman medical certificate for which you are making application.

3. FULL NAME -- If your name has changed for any reason, list current name on the application and list any former name(s) in the EXPLANATIONS box of number 18 on the application.

4. SOCIAL SECURITY NUMBER -- The social security number is optional; however, its use as a unique identifier does eliminate mistakes.

5. ADDRESS -- Give permanent mailing address and country. Include your complete nine digit ZIP code if known. Provide your current area code and telephone number.

6. DATE OF BIRTH -- Specify month (MM), day (DD), and year (YYYY) in numerals; e.g., 01/31/1950. Indicate citizenship; e.g., U.S.A.

7. COLOR OF HAIR -- Specify as brown, black, blond, gray, or red. If bald, so state. Do not abbreviate.

8. COLOR OF EYES -- Specify actual eye color as brown, black, blue, hazel, gray, or green. Do not abbreviate.

9. SEX -- Indicate male or female.

10. TYPE OF AIRMAN CERTIFICATE(S) YOU HOLD -- Check applicable block(s). If "Other" is checked, provide name of certificate.

11. OCCUPATION -- Indicate major employment. "Pilot" will be used only for those gaining their livelihood by flying.

12. EMPLOYER -- Provide your employer's full name. If self-employed, so state.

13. HAS YOUR FAA AIRMAN MEDICAL CERTIFICATE EVER BEEN DENIED, SUSPENDED, OR REVOKED -- If "yes" is checked, give month and year of action in numerals.

14. TOTAL PILOT TIME TO DATE -- Give total number of civilian flight hours. Indicate whether logged or estimated. Abbreviate as Log. or Est.

15. TOTAL PILOT TIME PAST 6 MONTHS -- Give number of civilian flight hours in the 6-month period immediately preceding date of this application. Indicate whether logged or estimated. Abbreviate as Log. or Est.

16. MONTH AND YEAR OF LAST FAA MEDICAL EXAMINATION -- Give month and year in numerals. If none, so state.

17a. DO YOU CURRENTLY USE ANY MEDICATION (Prescription or Nonprescription) -- Check "yes" or "no." If "yes" is checked, give name of medication(s) and indicate if the medication was listed in a previous FAA medical examination. See **NOTE** below.

17b. Indicate whether you use near vision contact lens(es) while flying.

18. MEDICAL HISTORY -- Each item under this heading must be checked either "yes" or "no." You must answer "yes" for every condition you have ever been diagnosed with, had, or presently have and describe the condition and approximate date in the EXPLANATIONS block.

If information has been reported on a previous application for airman medical certificate and there has been no change in your condition, you may note "PREVIOUSLY REPORTED, NO CHANGE" in the EXPLANATIONS box, but you must still check "yes" to the condition. Do not report occasional common illnesses such as colds or sore throats.

"Substance dependence" is defined by any of the following: increased tolerance; withdrawal symptoms; impaired control of use; or continued use despite damage to health or impairment of social, personal, or occupational functioning. "Substance abuse" includes the following: use of an illegal substance; use of a substance or substances in situations in which such use is physically hazardous; or misuse of a substance when such misuse has impaired health or social or occupational functioning. "Substances" include alcohol, PCP, marijuana, cocaine, amphetamines, barbiturates, opiates, and other psychoactive chemicals.

Conviction and/or Administrative Action History -- Letter (v) of this subheading asks if you have ever been: (1) convicted (which may include paying a fine, or forfeiting bond or collateral) of an offense involving driving while intoxicated by, while impaired by, or while under the influence of alcohol or a drug; or (2) convicted or subject to an administrative action by a state or other jurisdiction for an offense for which your license was denied, suspended, cancelled, or revoked or which resulted in attendance at an educational or rehabilitation program. Individual traffic convictions are not required to be reported if they did not involve: alcohol or a drug; suspension, revocation, cancellation, or denial of driving privileges; or attendance at an educational or rehabilitation program. If "yes" is checked, a description of the conviction(s) and/or administrative action(s) must be given in the EXPLANATIONS box. The description must include: (1) the alcohol or drug offense for which you were convicted or the type of administrative action involved (e.g., attendance at an alcohol treatment program in lieu of conviction; license denial, suspension, cancellation, or revocation for refusal to be tested; educational safe driving program for multiple speeding convictions; etc.); (2) the name of the state or other jurisdiction involved; and (3) the date of the conviction and/or administrative action. The FAA may check state motor vehicle driver licensing records to verify your responses. Letter (w) of this subheading asks if you have ever had any other (nontraffic) convictions (e.g., assault, battery, public intoxication, robbery, etc.). If so, name the charge for which you were convicted and the date of conviction in the EXPLANATIONS box. See **NOTE** below.

19. VISITS TO HEALTH PROFESSIONAL WITHIN LAST 3 YEARS -- List all visits in the last 3 years to a physician, physician assistant, nurse practitioner, psychologist, clinical social worker, or substance abuse specialist for treatment, examination, or medical/mental evaluation. List visits for counseling only if related to a personal substance abuse or psychiatric condition. Give date, name, address, and type of health professional consulted and briefly state reason for consultation. Multiple visits to one health professional for the same condition may be aggregated on one line. Routine dental, eye, and FAA periodic medical examinations and consultations with your employer-sponsored employee assistance program (EAP) may be excluded unless the consultations were for your substance abuse or unless the consultations resulted in referral for psychiatric evaluation or treatment. See **NOTE** below.

20. APPLICANT'S DECLARATION -- Two declarations are contained under this heading. The first authorizes the National Driver Register to release adverse driver history information, if any, about the applicant to the FAA. The second certifies the completeness and truthfulness of the applicant's responses on the medical application. The declaration section must be signed and dated by the applicant after the applicant has read it.

> **NOTE:** If more space is required to respond to "yes" answers for numbers 17, 18, or 19, use a plain sheet of paper bearing the information, your signature, and the date signed.

Applicant -- Please Tear Off This Sheet After Completing The Application Form.

Applicant Must Complete <u>ALL</u> 20 Items (Except For Shaded Areas) <u>PLEASE PRINT</u>   Form Approved OMB NO. 2120-0034

Copy of FAA Form 8500-8 (Medical Certificate) or FAA Form B420-2 Medical/Student Pilot Certificate) Issued. **FF- 1953420**	**1. Application For:** ☐ Airman Medical Certificate ☐ Airman Medical and Student Pilot Certificate	**2. Class of Medical Certificate Applied For:** ☐ 1st ☐ 2nd ☐ 3rd

MEDICAL CERTIFICATE _____ CLASS
AND STUDENT PILOT CERTIFICATE

This certifies that (*Full name and address*):

Date of Birth	Height	Weight	Hair	Eyes	Sex

has met the medical standards prescribed in Part 67, Federal Aviation Regulations, for this class of Medical Certificate

Limitations

Date of Examination   Examiner's Designation No.

Examiner   Signature

Typed Name

AIRMAN'S SIGNATURE

3. Last Name   **First Name**   **Middle Name**

4. Social Security Number ___ — ___ — ___

5. Address   Telephone Number ( )   -

Number/Street

City   State/Country   Zip Code

6. Date of Birth _____ M M / D D / Y Y Y Y

Citizenship _____

7. Color of Hair   **8. Color of Eyes**   **9. Sex**

10. Type of Airman Certificate(s) You Hold:
☐ None   ☐ ATC Specialist   ☐ Flight Instructor   ☐ Recreational
☐ Airline Transport   ☐ Flight Engineer   ☐ Private   ☐ Other
☐ Commercial   ☐ Flight Navigator   ☐ Student _____

11. Occupation   **12. Employer**

13. Has Your FAA Airman Medical Certificate Ever Been Denied, Suspended, or Revoked?
☐ Yes   ☐ No   If yes, give date _____ M M / D D / Y Y Y Y

Total Pilot Time (Civilian Only)   **16. Date of Last FAA Medical Application**
14. To Date   **15. Past 6 months**   _____ M M / D D / Y Y Y Y   ☐ No Prior Application

17a. Do You Currently Use Any Medication (Prescription or Nonprescription)?
☐ No   ☐ Yes (If yes, below list medication(s) used and check appropriate box)   Previously Reported   Yes No
_____ ☐ ☐
_____ ☐ ☐
_____ ☐ ☐
(If more space is required, see 17.a. on the instruction sheet).

17b. Do You Ever Use Near Vision Contact Lens(es) While Flying?   ☐ Yes ☐ No

18. Medical History - HAVE YOU EVER IN YOUR LIFE BEEN DIAGNOSED WITH, HAD, OR DO YOU PRESENTLY HAVE ANY OF THE FOLLOWING? Answer "yes" or "no" for every condition listed below. In the EXPLANATIONS box below, you may note "PREVIOUSLY REPORTED, NO CHANGE" only if the explanation of the condition was reported on a previous application for an airman medical certificate and there has been no change in your condition. **See Instructions Page**

Yes	No	Condition	Yes	No	Condition	Yes	No	Condition	Yes	No	Condition
a.☐	☐	Frequent or severe headaches	g.☐	☐	Heart or vascular trouble	m.☐	☐	Mental disorders of any sort: depression, anxiety, etc.	r. ☐	☐	Military medical discharge
b.☐	☐	Dizziness or fainting spell	h.☐	☐	High or low blood pressure	n. ☐	☐	Substance dependence or failed a drug test ever, or substance abuse or use of illegal substance in the last 2 years.	s.☐	☐	Medical rejection by military service
c.☐	☐	Unconsciousness for any reason	i. ☐	☐	Stomach, liver, or intestinal trouble				t. ☐	☐	Rejection for life or health insurance
d.☐	☐	Eye or vision trouble except glasses	j. ☐	☐	Kidney stone or blood in urine	o. ☐	☐	Alcohol dependence or abuse	u.☐	☐	Admission to hospital
e.☐	☐	Hay fever or allergy	k.☐	☐	Diabetes	p. ☐	☐	Suicide attempt	x.☐	☐	Other illness, disability, or surgery
f. ☐	☐	Asthma or lung disease	l. ☐	☐	Neurological disorders: epilepsy, seizures, stroke, paralysis, etc.	q.☐	☐	Motion sickness requiring medication			

Conviction and/or Administrative Action History -- See Instructions Page

Yes	No		Yes	No	
v. ☐	☐	History of (1) any conviction(s) involving driving while intoxicated by, while impaired by, or while under the influence of alcohol or a drug; or (2) history of any conviction(s) or administrative action(s) involving an offense(s) which resulted in the denial, suspension, cancellation, or revocation of driving privileges or which resulted in attendance at an educational or a rehabilitation program.	w.☐	☐	History of nontraffic conviction(s) (misdemeanors or felonies).

Explanations: See Instructions Page   FOR FAA USE
Review Action Codes

19.   Visits to Health Professional Within Last 3 Years.   ☐ Yes (explain below)   ☐ No   See Instructions Page

Date	Name, Address, and Type of Health Professional Consulted	Reason

-- NOTICE --
Whoever in any matter within the jurisdiction of any department or agency of the United States knowingly and willfully falsifies, conceals or covers up by any trick, scheme, or device a material fact, or who makes any false, fictitious, or fraudulent statements or representations, or entry, may be fined up to $250,000 or imprisoned not more than 5 years, or both, (18 U.S. Code Secs. 1001: 3571).

20. Applicant's National Driver Register and Certifying Declarations
I hereby authorize the National Driver Register (NDR), through a designated State Department of Motor Vehicles, to furnish to the FAA information pertaining to my driving record. This consent constitutes authorization for a single access to the information contained in the NDR to verify information provided in this application. Upon my request, the FAA shall make the information received from the NDR, if any, available for my review and written comment. Authority: 23 U.S. Code 401, Note.
NOTE: All persons using this form must sign it. NDR consent, however, does not apply unless this form is used as an application for Medical Certificate or Medical Certificate and Student Pilot Certificate.
I hereby certify that all statements and answers provided by me on this application form are complete and true to the best of my knowledge, and I agree that they are to be considered part of the basis for issuance of any FAA certificate to me. I have also read and understand the Privacy Act statement that accompanies this form.

Signature of Applicant   Date _____ M M / D D / Y Y Y Y

FAA Form 8500-8 (3-00) Supersedes Previous Edition   NSN-0052-00-670-6002

88

NOTE: FAA/Original Copy of the Report of Medical Examination Must Be TYPED.

REPORT OF MEDICAL EXAMINATION

21. Height (inches)	22. Weight (pounds)	23. Statement of Demonstrated Ability (SODA) ☐ Yes ☐ No Defect Noted:	24. SODA Serial Number

CHECK EACH ITEM IN APPROPRIATE COLUMN	Normal	Abnormal	CHECK EACH ITEM IN APPROPRIATE COLUMN	Normal	Abnormal
25. Head, face, neck, and scalp			37. Vascular system (Pulse, amplitude and character; arms, legs, others)		
26. Nose			38. Abdomen and viscera (Including hernia)		
27. Sinuses			39. Anus (Not including digital examination)		
28. Mouth and throat			40. Skin		
29. Ears, general (Internal and external canals; Hearing under item 49)			41. G-U system (Not including pelvic examination)		
30. Ear Drums (Perforation)			42. Upper and lower extremities (Strength and range of motion)		
31. Eyes, general (Vision under items 50 to 54)			43. Spine, other musculoskeletal		
32. Ophthalmoscopic			44. Identifying body marks, scars, tattoos (Size and location)		
33. Pupils (Equality and reaction)			45. Lymphatics		
34. Ocular motility (Associated parallel movement, nystagmus)			46. Neurologic (Tendon reflexes, equilibrium, senses, cranial nerves, coordination, etc.)		
35. Lungs and chest (Not including breasts examination)			47. Psychiatric (Appearance, behavior, mood, communication, and memory)		
36. Heart (Precordial activity, rhythm, sounds, and murmurs)			48. General systemic		

NOTES: Describe every abnormality in detail. Enter applicable item number before each comment. Use additional sheets if necessary and attach to this form.

49. Hearing

49. Hearing	Record Audiometric Speech Discrimination Score Below		Right Ear					Left Ear				
Conversational Voice Test at 6 Feet ☐ Pass ☐ Fail		Audiometer Threshold in Decibels	500	1000	2000	3000	4000	500	1000	2000	3000	4000

50. Distant Vision	51.a. Near Vision	51.b. Intermediate Vision - 32 Inches	52. Color Vision
Right 20/ Corrected to 20/ Left 20/ Corrected to 20/ Both 20/ Corrected to 20/	Right 20/ Corrected to 20/ Left 20/ Corrected to 20/ Both 20/ Corrected to 20/	Right 20/ Corrected to 20/ Left 20/ Corrected to 20/ Both 20/ Corrected to 20/	☐ Pass ☐ Fail

53. Field of Vision ☐ Normal ☐ Abnormal	54. Heterophoria 20' (in prism diopters)	Esophoria	Exophoria	Right Hyperphoria	Left Hyperphoria

55. Blood Pressure (Sitting, mm of Mercury)	Systolic	Diastolic /	56. Pulse (Resting)	57. Urinalysis (if abnormal, give results) ☐ Normal ☐ Abnormal	Albumin	Sugar	58. ECG (Date) M M D D Y Y Y Y

59. Other Tests Given

60. Comments on History and Findings: AME shall comment on all "YES" answers in the Medical History section and for abnormal findings of the examination. (Attach all consultation reports, ECGs, X-rays, etc. to this report before mailing.

FOR FAA USE

Pathology Codes:

Coded By:

Clerical Reject

Significant Medical History ☐ YES ☐ NO   **Abnormal Physical Findings** ☐ YES ☐ NO

61. Applicant's Name	62. Has Been Issued -- ☐ Medical Certificate ☐ Medical & Student Pilot Certificate ☐ **No Certificate Issued** -- Deferred for Further Evaluation ☐ **Has Been Denied** -- Letter of Denial Issued (Copy Attached)

63. Disqualifying Defects (List by item number)

64. Medical Examiner's Declaration -- I hereby certify that I have personally reviewed the medical history and personally examined the applicant named on this medical examination report. This report with any attachment embodies my findings completely and correctly.

Date of Examination M M D D Y Y Y Y	Aviation Medical Examiner's Name	Aviation Medical Examiner's Signature
	Street Address	AME Serial Number
	City State Zip Code	AME Telephone ( )

FAA Form 8500-8 (7-92) Supersedes Previous Editions

GLEIM® Pilot Kits

Sport Pilot	$199.95 _____
Private Pilot	$249.95 _____
Instrument Pilot	$249.95 _____
Commercial Pilot	$174.95 _____
Instrument/Commercial Pilot	$341.95 _____
Sport Pilot Flight Instructor	$174.95 _____
Flight/Ground Instructor	$174.95 _____
ATP	$189.95 _____

Also Available:

Flight Engineer Online Ground School	$99.95 _____
Flight Engineer Test Prep Software	$64.95 _____

Shipping (nonrefundable): **$20 per kit** $ _____
(Alaska and Hawaii please call for shipping price)
Add applicable sales tax for shipments within the state of Florida. $ _____
For orders outside the United States, please visit our website at
www.gleim.com/aviation/products.php to place your order.   TOTAL $ _____

Reference Materials and Other Accessories Available by Contacting Gleim.

TOLL FREE: 800.874.5346 ext. 471 WEBSITE: gleim.com	LOCAL: 352.375.0772 ext. 471 FAX: 352.375.6940 EMAIL: sales@gleim.com	Gleim Publications, Inc. P.O. Box 12848 Gainesville, FL 32604

NAME (please print) _____

ADDRESS_____ Apt. _____
          (street address required for UPS)

_____

CITY _____ STATE _____ ZIP _____

_____ MC/VISA/DISC _____ Check/M.O.   Daytime Telephone (_____) ____ - _____

Credit Card # _____ - _____ - _____ - _____

Exp. ____ / ____   Signature _____
        Mo./Yr.

Email Address _____

1. We process and ship orders daily, within one business day over 98.8% of the time. Call by 3:00 pm for same day service.
2. Gleim Publications, Inc. guarantees the immediate refund of all resalable texts, unopened and un-downloaded Test Prep Software, and unopened audios returned within 30 days. Online courses may be canceled within 30 days if no more than the first study unit or lesson has been accessed. This only applies to products that are purchased directly from Gleim Publications, Inc. No refunds will be provided on opened or downloaded Test Prep Software or audios, partial returns of package sets, or shipping and handling charges. Any freight charges incurred for returned or refused packages will be the customer's responsibility.
3. Please PHOTOCOPY this order form for others.
4. No CODs. Orders from individuals must be prepaid.
5. Shipping and handling charges are nonrefundable.

Prices subject to change without notice.   3/11

Please forward your suggestions, corrections, and comments concerning typographical errors, etc., to **Irvin N. Gleim • c/o Gleim Publications, Inc. • P.O. Box 12848 • University Station • Gainesville, Florida • 32604.** Please include your name and address so we can properly thank you for your interest.

1. _____

2. _____

3. _____

4. _____

5. _____

6. _____

7. _____

8. _____

9. _____

10. _____

11. _____

12. _____

13. _____

14. _____

15. _____

16. _____

17. _____

18. _____

Remember, for superior service: Email, mail, or fax questions about our materials.
                                  Telephone questions about orders, prices, shipments, or payments.

Name: _____

Address: _____

City/State/Zip: _____

Telephone: Home: _____ Work: _____ Fax: _____

Email: _____